W9-BMD-257

GREAT BRITISH COOKING:
A WELL-KEPT SECRET

LIBRARY
LINCOLN MEMORIAL UNIVERSITY
Harrogate, Tennessee 37752

Great British Cooking: A Well-Kept Secret

by Jane Garmey

Foreword by Calvin Trillin

112843

RANDOM HOUSE 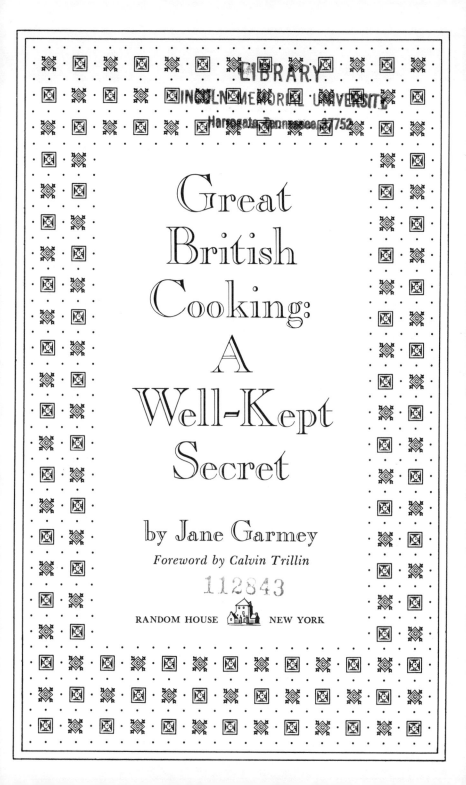 NEW YORK

TX717
G32

Copyright © 1981 by Jane Garmey
All rights reserved under International and
Pan-American Copyright Conventions. Published in the
United States by Random House, Inc., New York,
and simultaneously in Canada by Random House of
Canada Limited, Toronto.

Library of Congress Cataloging in Publication Data
Garmey, Jane.
Great British cooking, a well kept secret.
Includes index.
1. Cookery, British.   I. Title.
TX717.G32   641.5941   81-40247
ISBN 0-394-50876-9   AACR2

Manufactured in the United States of America
24689753
First Edition

Book design: Elissa Ichiyasu

FOR STEPHEN AND EDWARD

Foreword BY CALVIN TRILLIN

"It's certainly unfair to say that the English lack both a cuisine and a sense of humor," I said, as we were about to leave for Jane Garmey's house to try an authentic English meal. "Their cooking is a joke in itself."

"I suppose you've prepared for this dinner party by polishing remarks like that all day," my wife, Alice, said, using the voice she employs to indicate that she is resigned to being embarrassed by my behavior yet again.

"Only partly," I said. "I have also taken the precaution of eating dinner. Do you think they'll have a crane?"

"A crane?" Alice said. "I've never heard of anybody eating crane."

"Not that sort of crane," I said. "A hydraulic crane for lifting the dessert. Haven't you ever seen them serve one of those 'trifles' at an English café? 'A little to the left, Alfie. That's it. Lower away. Steady as she goes.' Why do you think I try to avoid restaurants in London where the waiters are wearing hard hats?"

"I'm sure this meal is going to be a lot better than you expect," Alice said.

"Well, I was definitely encouraged by the fact that the date was agreed upon only two weeks in advance," I said. "Jane really hasn't had time to give the vegetables a proper English boil. Well brought up English girls are taught by their mothers to boil all veggies for at least a month and a half, just in case one of the dinner guests turns up without his teeth."

"You know very well that Jane is a marvelous cook," Alice said. "She's planning to publish an English cookbook."

"Has she exhibited other self-destructive tendencies in the past?"

"The kind of food you hate so much in England is not really English food," Alice said.

It's true that I find the English version of "continental cuisine" particularly loathsome. It consists of stuffing something with something else and covering the resulting atrocity with a viscous goo. I call it Stuff Stuff with Heavy. I wouldn't be surprised to learn that someone in the Stuff Stuff with Heavy crowd had at some point stuffed a crane with something else or even stuffed something else with a crane. "I always say that with their own food the English are at least fair-minded enough to label the crime," I said. "In a way, anybody who eats something called Toad in the Hole or Bosworth Jumbles deserves what he gets."

"Yes, you always do say that," Alice said. "Maybe you could avoid saying it just for this evening, and then begin saying it again early tomorrow morning."

"Well, at least we might find out from Jane what Priddy Oggy with Scrumpy Sauce is," I said, trying to look on the bright side. Once, while driving through Somerset, we found ourselves within a few miles of a restaurant that was identified in the guidebook as specializing in something called Priddy Oggy with Scrumpy Sauce. Hurrying in that direction, I was tormented with thoughts of how we might be denied the opportunity of at least seeing what Priddy Oggy with Scrumpy Sauce looked like on the plate (I was not committed to eating any). The waiter, I feared, might say "The Oggy's finished" or "We no longer do Priddy Oggy" or "The only Scrumpy Sauce we've got is the tinned." We arrived to find the restaurant closed—meaning that we seemed fated never to know even whether Priddy Oggy is a main course or something requiring a hydraulic delivery system.

"You love Cornish pasties," Alice said. "You love scones. You love the hog's pudding we buy at the Barnstaple market. You love those huge English breakfasts."

I do cherish breakfast in England. In fact, I have always assumed that the English seem so down in the mouth all the time because they have to go through life realizing every morning before nine that breakfast is over and the rest of the day is bound to be downhill. "You don't think Jane might serve breakfast, do you?" I asked Alice. "I mean with the time difference and all."

"There's something wrong here," I whispered to Alice when we were halfway through the meal. The main course did indeed have one of those English names—something like Aunt Becky's Kneecap—but it was delicious. Although I was loath to accuse Jane of not having an English sense of history, the vegetables did not, in fact, taste as if they had been cooking since the Wars of the Roses. The hostess herself, a mere slip of a thing, easily carried dessert to the table with one hand.

"Maybe it's not really English," I whispered, as we were eating dessert. Was it possible that Jane Garmey had simply given real food an English name—the way someone might fit out a Rumanian with a regimental blazer and call him Nigel? In the weeks following our dinner, that suspicion faded as reports came in from others who had sampled and loved dishes with names like Cullen Skink and Soles in Their Coffins. I have finally been forced to face the possibility that Jane Garmey knows how to make English food that tastes good. If hidden away in some cupboard in the Garmey household is a French cookbook that has a recipe for something called *La Rotule de Tante Becky*, I've been had. Otherwise, my conclusion about Jane Garmey and English cooking is this: She doesn't really know what Priddy Oggy with Scrumpy Sauce * is, but she knows everything else.

* Not so! For a detailed explanation of Priddy Oggy (not to be confused with Tiddy Oggy), see page 239. The recipe for Scrumpy Sauce can be found on page 146.

Contents

Introduction

It is widely held that British cuisine is a dubious affair. As Mrs. Ramsay said, in Virginia Woolf's *To the Lighthouse,*

"What passes for cookery in England is an abomination. . . . It is putting cabbages in water. It is roasting meat till it is like leather. It is cutting off the delicious skins of vegetables."

"In which," said Mr. Bankes, "all the virtue of the vegetable is contained."

"And the waste," said Mrs. Ramsay. "A whole French family could live on what an English cook throws away."

This view, while not entirely unwarranted, is nevertheless a caricature. British food like British weather has, in fact, been much maligned. Most visitors to Britain do manage to regard the weather with a kind of benign tolerance, believing, despite the rain, in those famous "bright periods" forever scheduled for some other part of the country. The same visitors, on the other hand, become quite vitriolic about British food, reporting it to be generally inedible, turning it into the helpless target of their scorn and the butt of endless jokes. British cooking has acquired what might be termed a serious image problem. This is particularly unfortunate because it is often quite superb. What presents the real problem for the foreign visitor is that it is hard to find.

British cooking is a phenomenon of the home, not generally available in hotels and restaurants, and the British home, be it castle or cottage, is definitely more impregnable than its American counterpart.

The British, for the most part, are not quick to make new friends; they distrust strangers, feel more at ease with formal introductions and prefer to "break the ice gently." This makes it difficult for most foreign tourists ever to gain entrance to an actual home and discover that there is more to British cooking than frozen cod steaks, stodge and overcooked cabbage.

Few visitors have ever tasted the delights of a Bakewell Tart, of Cornish Pasties, Marbled Veal or Angels on Horseback. The British, for their part, have now taken so much abuse for what passes as their native cuisine that they have become defensive and self-conscious on the subject, and many have even come to believe that enjoyment of their own cooking is an ethnic eccentricity. In addition, having what is generally regarded as the world's most sophisticated cuisine at their doorstep—the coast of France is less than twenty miles from the cliffs of Dover —has done nothing to help the matter.

It goes almost without saying that in this century the French have established preeminence in the art of cooking, but this was not always so. A spirited rivalry between the cooks of England and France dates back to the Middle Ages. At a banquet dinner given by Cardinal Wolsey in 1527, George Cavendish, who was his usher and later his biographer, wrote in his diary: "I suspect the French never saw the like." And while the French influence on the British kitchen was particularly strong in the seventeenth century after Charles II and his court returned from exile across the channel, by the middle of the following century a prominent English cookery text warned its readers that "if gentlemen will have French cooks, they must pay for French tricks . . . so much is the blind folly of this age that they would rather be imposed on by a French booby than give encouragement to a good English cook."

In the nineteenth century, the great French chef Carême trained at the Royal Pavilion, Brighton, under the shade of those famous metal palm trees that support its kitchen ceiling. Indeed, a number of other prominent French cooks such as Soyer and Escoffier worked in England and many recipes that people assume to be French have their British counterparts, if not originals. For instance, Crème Brûlée appears quite early as Burnt Cream, and Poor Knights of Windsor is very similar to the French recipe Pain Perdu. However, since cooks are notorious borrowers and thieves, all that this really proves is that no cuisine belongs exclusively to one country. What each country does is to lend food a national character.

British cookery comes from a tradition of domestic cooking. (Incidentally, throughout the book when I refer to "British" food, I am implying food that is served anywhere in the British Isles; "English" pertains to that which predominates only in England.) Not surprisingly, the great cookery writers have all been women: Hannah Glasse, Elizabeth Raffald, Maria Rundell, Eliza Acton and, of course, the incomparable Isabella Beeton, whose *Book of Household Management,* published in 1861, presents an unparalleled guide to the manners, economies and eating habits of the Victorian household. When one realizes that she was the oldest of twenty-one children and died at the age of twenty-eight, following the birth of her fourth child, her achievement seems even more remarkable.

The British cuisine is substantial, for the British are large eaters and believe in four meals a day. At its best, it is a cuisine that is simple, plain and wholesome. Traditional recipes are usually neither subtle nor elaborate; they tend to be practical and uncomplicated and require good raw materials: tender meat, fresh fish and vegetables in season. Rosa Lewis, the proprietress of the Cavendish Hotel and the model for Louisa Trotter in the television series *The Duchess of Duke Street,* expressed this very succinctly in a letter written to the *Times* in 1950:

> Good plain cooking is really the best and the best requires no trimmings. My idea of plain cooking is that whenever possible, the article should be cooked when in season and should not be cut up. Let the potato or the truffle stand on its own and be eaten whole.

British cooking has naturally been affected by traditions and tastes from different parts of the British empire: teas from Ceylon and Chutney, Kedgeree and Mulligatawny soup from India. It has also been influenced by that formidable institution, the British nanny. Her nursery favorites such as Bread and Butter Pudding, Spotted Dick and Treacle Tart all hold their place in the domain of British cooking.

Since real British cooking exists primarily within the home and restaurants rarely dare to compete, the British have developed a strange affinity for dining out in foreign restaurants. Unable, for the most part, to judge the merits and subtleties of an unfamiliar cuisine, they naïvely assume that the food must be good even when it tastes quite appalling. Meanwhile, in the kitchen at home, the native cuisine remains a well-kept secret, practiced and passed on to successive generations with little or no fanfare. Like many an ethnic cuisine, its livelihood has at times seemed threatened, but in recent years there has been a renewed interest in the art of traditional cooking. Old recipes are being rediscovered and restaurants are even beginning to sneak onto their menus such dishes as Sussex Pond Pudding, Hindle Wakes, Cockie Leekie and Syllabub. British cooking may even be in danger of becoming fashionable.

Most British recipes are easily adapted to the American kitchen. Regrettably omitted from this book are those with ingredients not readily available here, dishes such as Fidget Pie, which calls for two larks, Partridges in their Nightshirts and Jugged Hare.

The collection of recipes I have assembled is in no way comprehensive or complete; it is a personal collection that draws on a number of early cookery books, on my own subjective taste and on the suggestions and ideas of friends. Without their help and in many cases their generous offers of favorite recipes, the book could not have been written. In particular, I would like to thank Robert Abel, Rosemary Bett, Diana Bourdrez, Penelope Burns, Juliet Crump, Esther de Waal, Mary Jane Drummond, Peter ffrench Hodges, Kay Heymann, Joan and Peg Jackson, Susan Newall, Frances O'Malley, Patrick Rance, Rachel Ryan, Willard Taylor and Hugh Van Dusen. Special thanks are also due to Charlotte Sheedy, who first encouraged me with this venture.

Breakfast

Porridge
Kippers
Creamed Finnan Haddie
Kedgeree
Bacon, Tomatoes and Fried Bread
Fishcakes
Oxford Sausages
Deviled Kidneys
Bacon Fraize

Many visitors to Britain find breakfast a meal of astonishing dimensions. Actually, however, it has been in somewhat of a decline for the past sixty-five years and is nowhere near the size and variety it used to be in Victorian and Edwardian times.

In those days, it was not uncommon to come downstairs and find the sideboard laden with an array of chafing dishes containing such offerings as deviled kidneys, scrambled eggs, kedgeree, potted meat, cold grouse and kippers, as well as porridge, toast, rolls, two or three different kinds of marmalade, jams, jellies, fruit and, of course, tea.

In the eighteenth century big breakfasts were a rural phenomenon and essentially a masculine affair, being consumed in the late morning by the gentlemen of the household after their return from several hours of riding, shooting or fishing. Scottish breakfasts were reputed to be even more elaborate and gargantuan than their English counterparts and Dr. Johnson is credited with saying, "The way to eat well in Scotland is to eat breakfast three times a day."

The Victorians transformed it into a family meal and began to eat it earlier. (Empire builders couldn't dally all morning at their food.) Even in those days, when there was an abundance of servants, it was always the custom at breakfast to serve yourself directly from the sideboard. Possibly this was because people arrived at different times or because the servants were eating their own breakfast at the same time, but it is more likely that it was because the task of bringing at least eight dishes to the table for each person would have been exceedingly cumbersome. The Edwardians continued the tradition of the large, social breakfast. It was not until the First World War that the meal, along with parlormaids and footmen, suffered a decline.

By the time of the Second World War, breakfast as the Edwardians knew it had almost completely vanished. Today, the standard British breakfast is limited to cereal, followed by some combination of eggs, bacon, sausages, tomatoes and fried bread and finishing up with toast, marmalade and tea. Still a not inconsiderable meal, but hardly what it once was!

The secret of the English breakfast is the combination of tastes and flavors. A grilled tomato on its own is good, but served in conjunction with bacon and fried bread, it can become extraordinary. Eggs and bacon is probably the most popular breakfast combination, but especially on weekends, when there is time to read the papers and linger over one's food, it is worth recovering some of the dishes that so delighted the Edwardians.

◨ Porridge

Porridge is Scotland's immortal contribution to the British breakfast. The Scots take their porridge very seriously and many Scottish cooks insist that it must be made with fresh spring water, served in a wooden bowl and eaten with a horn spoon. Whether or not you go to these extremes, Porridge should be served with a little cream or milk and a sprinkling of sugar. *Serves 4.*

4½ cups water
¾ cup oatmeal
¼ teaspoon salt

Bring the water to a rapid boil in a saucepan and then sprinkle in the oatmeal. Stir with a spoon until the oatmeal has been absorbed and the mixture returns to a boil.

Cover and simmer gently for about 30 minutes, stirring from time to time. If it seems too stiff, add a little more hot water.

Add the salt and serve hot.

◫ Kippers

Kippers were first made in Scotland and have become something of a national industry. However, Canadian kippers, which are easier to find in the United States, are usually excellent, too. Canned kippers are suitable for a recipe like <u>Kipper Pâté</u>,* but I would not recommend them on their own for breakfast.

Allow one kipper per person and trim off the heads and tails. Kippers can either be grilled or cooked by the "jug" method. *To grill:* Brush the kipper with melted butter and place it under the broiler for about 3 minutes on each side. Remove and serve with a pat of butter on top.

To prepare by the jug method: Fill a large pitcher with boiling water and immerse the kipper in the water for 5 minutes. Drain and serve with a pat of butter. The advantage of this method is that it reduces the strong kipper smell, which tends to linger. On the other hand, there is nothing that quite compares with a grilled kipper.

* All underscored items are recipes given elsewhere in the book and may be looked up in the Index.

▨ Creamed Finnan Haddie

This dish takes its name from the fishing village of Findon in Kincardineshire, Scotland, where the fishermen's wives originated the now-famous method of smoking haddock by hanging it salted in their chimneys over a peat fire. While Finnan Haddie is delicious for breakfast, it also makes a good light supper dish. *Serves 6.*

2 pounds smoked haddock
1 small onion, finely chopped
8 peppercorns
3 cups milk
Juice of half a lemon
1 sprig parsley
3 cups Parsley Sauce

Wash the fish and cut it into smallish pieces. Place these in a shallow, heavy pan. Sprinkle the onion and peppercorns over the fish and add the milk, lemon juice and parsley. Cover with a close-fitting lid and poach the fish very slowly until it is just cooked (approximately 10 minutes).

Remove the fish from the liquor and skin and bone it. Arrange it in a serving dish, cover and keep warm.

Follow the instructions for making Parsley Sauce, substituting for Chicken Stock the liquor in which the haddock has been cooked.

Pour the sauce over the haddock and serve with toast.

◩ Kedgeree

Kedgeree is one of the best known of all Anglo-Indian recipes. Although it is traditionally served for breakfast, there is no reason not to have it for lunch or dinner. *Serves 4–6.*

1 pound smoked haddock fillets
2 tablespoons oil
1 large onion, finely chopped
1 cup long-grain rice
1 teaspoon curry powder
2 ounces butter
3 hard-boiled eggs, chopped into small pieces
½ cup chopped parsley
1 lemon, cut into thin round slices

Place the haddock in a shallow heavy pan and cover it with boiling water. Cook over low heat for about 10 minutes, or until the flesh is soft. Do not let the water come to a boil again; it should only simmer.

Remove the haddock and reserve the cooking water. Discard any skin or bones and flake the fish into pieces no larger than 1 inch.

Pour the oil into a saucepan and gently sauté the onion for a couple of minutes. Add the rice, and as soon as it becomes transparent, stir in the curry powder. Take 2½ cups of the water in which the fish was cooked and pour it over the onion and curry mixture. Cook gently until the rice is tender and the water has been absorbed (approximately 15 minutes). Check the rice from time to time to make sure that it does not stick; it may be necessary to add a few more tablespoons of water if it seems to be getting too dry.

When the rice is cooked, add the fish and the butter. Turn into a hot serving dish. Mix in the eggs and the parsley.

Decorate with the lemon slices before serving.

◳ Bacon, Tomatoes and Fried Bread

This is my favorite of all breakfast dishes, provided you can get real, ripe tomatoes. I could happily eat it at any time of the day. *Serves 4.*

4 medium-sized fresh tomatoes, cut in half
1 ounce butter
8 bacon slices
4 thick slices bread, crusts removed

Place the tomatoes in a pan, dot them with butter and cook them under the broiler until they are tender but not soggy (about 5 minutes).

In the meantime, cook the bacon in a frying pan and when it is done, transfer it to a serving dish and keep warm. Turn up the heat and place the bread in the same frying pan. Fry the bread until it is golden on both sides and serve immediately with the tomatoes and the bacon.

▧ Fishcakes

Fishcakes have fallen into ill repute, and the makers of frozen foods must accept the brunt of the blame. Mass-produced fish-cakes are really dreadful, so bad in fact that many people have absolutely no idea how delicious homemade ones can be. They are especially good for breakfast and can be prepared a day ahead of time, so that all you have to do in the morning is fry them. *Serves 4.*

1 pound cooked whitefish (cod, flounder, perch)
2 cups cooked mashed potatoes
1 raw egg
1 hard-boiled egg, chopped into small pieces
¼ teaspoon lemon juice
¼ teaspoon tarragon vinegar
1 tablespoon chopped parsley
Salt
Freshly ground black pepper
Flour
4 tablespoons stale breadcrumbs

Flake the fish and remove any bones. Combine it in a mixing bowl with the mashed potato and raw egg. When well mixed, add the hard-boiled egg, lemon juice, vinegar and parsley. Season well with salt and pepper.

The mixture will now be rather sticky and should be shaped into little round cakes. To do this, dip your fingers in flour. Roll each cake in breadcrumbs, cover and refrigerate for at least 2 hours.

When ready to serve, fry each fishcake in a little hot oil in a frying pan over medium heat (or if you prefer you can deep fry them). They should be both golden and crisp on the outside. Serve immediately.

▣ Oxford Sausages

There is something almost legendary about the English sausage or banger, as it is usually called. However, the dismal truth is that finding an English butcher who still makes his or her own sausages is no simple matter.

Oxford sausages, which date back to the eighteenth century, are still sold in Oxford and traditionally are made from equal parts of veal and pork. Since they are skinless, they are very simple to prepare and, so long as they are refrigerated, they can be made ahead of time and heated up at the last moment. *Serves 4.*

8 ounces ground veal
8 ounces ground pork
1 cup shredded or finely chopped suet
Grated rind of one lemon
1 cup fresh breadcrumbs
¼ teaspoon grated nutmeg
1 teaspoon sage
Pinch of thyme, savory and marjoram
1 teaspoon salt
Freshly ground black pepper
2 egg yolks

Mix all the ingredients except the egg yolks together, then bind the mixture with the yolks. Roll into sausage shapes and fry in a little butter for approximately 10 minutes, turning frequently.

◪ Deviled Kidneys

This was a favorite dish of the Edwardians. *Serves 4.*

8 kidneys, cut into small cubes
1 tablespoon flour
Salt
Cayenne pepper
2 tablespoons prepared English mustard
2 ounces butter
1½ teaspoons Worcestershire sauce
½ cup Chicken Stock
4 slices hot buttered toast

Dust the kidneys with flour and a sprinkling of salt and cayenne pepper and roll them in the mustard.

Melt the butter in a small frying pan and cook the kidneys over low heat for 5 minutes, turning them from time to time.

Pour on the Worcestershire sauce and the Chicken Stock and simmer uncovered until the gravy thickens. Serve on hot buttered toast.

⊠ Bacon Fraize

An old English recipe for quick, simple breakfast pancakes. *Serves 4.*

6 bacon slices, cut into small squares
⅔ cup flour
1 egg
½ cup plus 2 tablespoons milk
Salt

Fry the bacon in a small frying pan.

Place the flour in a mixing bowl. Beat in the egg and gradually add the milk, beating until there are no lumps. Add a pinch of salt.

When the bacon is almost cooked, remove it from the pan and divide it into 4 portions. Wipe the excess fat from the pan and replace 1 portion of bacon. Pour into the pan one quarter of the batter and cook over medium heat until the underneath is firm, then turn and cook the other side. Roll up the pancake or fold it in half and transfer it to a serving dish. Cook the remaining pancakes in the same manner. Serve immediately.

Soups

Chicken Stock
Meat Stock
Almond Soup
Chestnut Soup
Partan Bree
Cullen Skink
Mussel Soup
Queen Victoria's Soup
Whitefish Soup with Green Speckled Fishballs
Mulligatawny Soup
Cockie Leekie
Highland Pheasant Soup
Brown Windsor Soup
Scotch Broth
Oxtail Soup
Diana's Lamb Soup
Cold Pease Soup
Tomato Soup
Orange Carrot Soup
Hampshire Cream Soup
Saxe-Coburg Soup
Turnip Soup
Cawl Mamgu
Winter Vegetable Soup

The arrival of food processors and blenders has changed soup making from an arduous chore to a quick and simple undertaking, and soup has become very popular again. From Norman times to the eighteenth century, soup was the main meal of the day for the poor. (The word soup comes from *sop*—a term used for a piece of bread dipped or soaked in some kind of broth.) Many Victorian cookery books contain elaborate instructions on how to prepare large quantities of soup for the poor, and it was the custom for the ladies of the household to distribute soup regularly to the deserving masses.

There is a tragic old Cornish recipe, called Sky Blue and Sinkers, for a soup to be served to children during time of famine. It was made by mixing a little flour with skimmed milk and pouring it into a large amount of boiling water. This broth would be ladled into individual bowls, each containing a piece of bread that would rise to the surface and then sink to the bottom so that only the pale blue of the watery milk would be visible.

However, soup was not limited to the poor. In Elizabethan times, pottages containing whole birds or large pieces of meat were common fare, and almond soup and hare soup were particular favorites. By the nineteenth century soup had become the proper way to begin a dinner, and both those great ladies of Victorian cookery, Mrs. Beeton and Eliza Acton, have numerous recipes for hearty meat soups as well as the more delicately flavored vegetable and fish soups. The most sought-after soup of the day was real turtle soup, which is still served at the annual Lord Mayor's banquet. Since it was a very elaborate, expensive soup that took the better part of two days to prepare, mock turtle soup, which used a calf's head instead of a turtle, was an acceptable substitute. If even that was too much of a chore, you could settle for an imitation mock turtle soup made from Meat Stock, flavored with Madeira and turtle herbs.

Obviously, soup should always be made with homemade stock if possible. However, if you are in a hurry, who can deny the virtue of the bouillon cube, which, incidentally, is not even a twentieth-century invention. The Victorians had bouillon cubes, which they called "portable soup." They were made by boiling stock until it turned into a kind of stiff glue, which was then cut into squares and kept for many years. Portable soup was very popular with sailors and explorers, and Captain Cook even took a good supply of it with him on his first voyage to Australia.

▣ Chicken Stock

Makes 4½ cups.

Bones and carcass of a cooked chicken
Chicken giblets
1 carrot, sliced
2 sticks celery, sliced
1 medium-sized onion, stuck with 3 cloves
2 tablespoons parsley
½ teaspoon thyme
1 bayleaf
1 teaspoon salt
6 peppercorns
6 cups water

Put all the ingredients in a large saucepan. Bring to a boil and skim off any scum. Cover and simmer over very low heat for two hours.

Strain the liquid into a bowl or jar. Allow the stock to cool and remove any fat before using. The stock should be refrigerated until needed. It should not be kept in the refrigerator for more than 3 to 4 days but it can be frozen for up to 6 months.

▣ Meat Stock

Makes 6½ cups.

2–3 pounds meat bones
3 sticks celery, sliced
2 medium-sized onions, stuck with 4 cloves
1 carrot, sliced
2 tablespoons parsley
½ teaspoon thyme
1 bayleaf
8 peppercorns
8 cups water

Follow the instructions for making Chicken Stock.

◈ Almond Soup

In medieval times, almond milk—an infusion of ground almonds and sweetened broth or wine—was used as a substitute
for cows' milk on fasting days. As the fasting laws relaxed and
this need diminished, the recipe evolved into a rich, thick,
white soup with a milk-and-cream base. Almond soup can be
served either chilled or hot, but since it is very rich the portions
should be small. *Serves 6.*

1¼ cups ground almonds
6 cups Chicken Stock
½ teaspoon white pepper
1 bayleaf
1 ounce butter
1 tablespoon cornstarch
2 cups milk
1 cup heavy cream
½ cup sherry
Salt
¼ cup slivered almonds

Put the ground almonds with the stock, pepper and bayleaf in
a saucepan. Bring to a boil and simmer covered for 30 minutes.
Remove the bayleaf and puree the soup in a blender or food
processor.

Melt the butter in a separate saucepan over low heat. Add the
cornstarch, cook for 1 minute and then gradually add the milk,
stirring constantly. When the milk is fully absorbed, stir in the
almond puree. Add the cream and sherry and season to taste
with salt. Continue to simmer the soup for another 10 minutes but be careful not to allow it to boil.

Sauté the slivered almonds in a little butter until they are
golden brown and scatter them over the soup just before
serving.

◈ Chestnut Soup

Mrs. Hannah Glasse in *The Art of Cookery Made Plain and Simple,* published in 1747, has a recipe for Chestnut Soup that calls for "half a hundred chestnuts." Other ingredients include 3 pigeons, ham, veal and a few other more mundane items. My version, based on a recipe contributed in 1935 to *The Farmers Weekly* by a Mrs. Chell of Essex, is rather simpler. *Serves 6.*

1 pound chestnuts
5 cups Chicken Stock
2 cups milk
¼ teaspoon mace
Salt
Freshly ground black pepper

To skin the chestnuts: Make a cut along the flat side of each chestnut and drop it into a pan of boiling salted water. Let the chestnuts boil for 5 minutes and then take out 2 or 3 at a time (as they have to be peeled hot) and remove both the outer shells and inner skins.

Simmer the peeled chestnuts for 10 to 15 minutes in a fresh pan of water until they are tender; do not overcook or they will fall apart.

Puree the chestnuts in a blender or food processor and put them in another saucepan. Add the stock, milk and mace. Season to taste, reheat and serve.

◙ Partan Bree

A delicious, thick, creamy crab soup from Scotland: *partan* is the Gaelic word for crab and *bree* comes from *brigh,* which means broth. *Serves 4–6.*

3 cups milk
1 cup rice
3 anchovy fillets
½ pound fresh cooked crabmeat (frozen or canned crabmeat may be substituted)
3 cups Chicken Stock
Salt
Freshly ground black pepper
1 cup heavy cream

Bring the milk almost to the boiling point in a heavy-bottomed saucepan. Add the rice and anchovy fillets. Simmer until the rice is well done. Remove from the heat and add the crabmeat.

Puree the soup in a blender or food processor. Return the pureed soup to a large saucepan and gradually stir in the stock. Season with salt and pepper to taste. Add the cream just before serving.

N.B.: This soup can be served either hot or cold. For some reason, it always seems to taste better hot.

◪ Cullen Skink

This Scottish smoked haddock soup has a wonderful golden color and a marvelous smoky flavor. *Skink* is a Gaelic word meaning essence. *Serves 6.*

1½ pounds smoked haddock fillets
2 cups milk
1 medium-sized onion, finely chopped
3½ cups water
1 cup diced raw potato
1 ounce butter
1 cup heavy cream
Salt
Freshly ground black pepper
½ cup chopped parsley

Put the smoked haddock in a large, shallow pan with the milk, onion and water. Bring slowly to a boil and remove from the heat. Lift the fish out of the pan, skin and bone it and flake it into small pieces, then set aside. Place the skin and bones in a saucepan with the cooking liquid and the onion. Add the potato and simmer for one hour.

Strain the stock through a sieve and return it to the saucepan. Heat thoroughly and add the fish, butter and cream. Season to taste with salt and pepper and sprinkle the parsley over the top just before serving.

◩ Mussel Soup

Creamy and subtle, this soup should be saved for special occasions. It makes the perfect beginning to an elegant meal. *Serves 6.*

1½ quarts mussels (about 35 mussels)
2 cups dry white wine
1 cup water
3 ounces butter
2 medium-sized onions, finely chopped
1 garlic clove, crushed
2 tablespoons flour
2 cups milk
Salt
Freshly ground black pepper
½ teaspoon nutmeg
1 tablespoon lemon juice
1 cup heavy cream
¼ cup chopped parsley

Scrub and de-beard the mussels under cold running water, using a stiff brush. Do not use any that are broken or that have already opened up.

Put the mussels in a large kettle with the wine and water. Cover and bring to a boil. Continue to boil for about 5 minutes, shaking the pan from time to time.

When the mussels have all opened up, remove the kettle from the heat. Take the mussels out of their shells and place them in a sieve over a bowl. Add the juices left in the kettle to those in the bowl and re-strain through a very fine sieve or a piece of cheesecloth.

Melt the butter in a good-sized heavy saucepan. Add the onions and garlic and cook until golden. Add the flour and gradually pour in the milk, stirring all the time so as to make a smooth sauce. Be careful not to let the sauce boil. Finally, add the strained juices and season with salt, pepper and nutmeg.

Just before serving add the mussels, lemon juice and cream. Reheat the soup very gently: Do not allow it even to simmer or the mussels will become tough and stringy. Sprinkle with parsley before serving. Mussel Soup may be served hot or cold.

◪ Queen Victoria's Soup

This soup is believed to have been one of Queen Victoria's favorites and was frequently to be found on the menu whenever she stayed at Balmoral Castle. The original recipe calls for veal stock, not Chicken Stock. However, I have substituted the latter for convenience since it does not significantly alter the taste. *Serves 8.*

1 chicken (3–5 pounds), or 2 small chickens, cut up
8 cups Chicken Stock
1 bunch parsley
3 cups fresh breadcrumbs
4 cups heavy cream
3 hard-boiled egg yolks, minced

Put the chicken in a large saucepan. Cover with the stock and parsley. Bring to a boil, cover and simmer for 1 hour.

Lift the chicken and the parsley out of the saucepan. Skin and bone the chicken and cut the meat into small pieces.

Add the breadcrumbs and the cut-up chicken to the broth. Mix in the cream and the minced yolks. Adjust the seasoning if necessary. Reheat, being careful not to boil, and serve.

112843

⊠ Whitefish Soup with Green Speckled Fishballs

This dish is adapted from a recipe given by Lady Sarah Lindsay in her book *A Few Choice Recipes,* published in 1883. Do not be put off by its rather prosaic name for it is really quite special. The speckled fishballs float in the soup and look exotic, and the unusual combination of textures makes this a soup for a grand occasion. *Serves 6.*

¾ pound fillet of cod or perch
3 parsley stalks
¾ cup white wine
4 cups water
2 ounces butter
4 tablespoons flour
Salt
Freshly ground black pepper
1 cup light cream
FOR THE FISHBALLS:
¼ pound fillet of cod or perch
1 anchovy
2 tablespoons fresh white breadcrumbs
¼ teaspoon cayenne pepper
1 egg
2 tablespoons finely chopped fresh parsley

Put the fish in a saucepan with the parsley stalks, wine and water. Cover and bring to a boil, then simmer for 15 minutes.

During this time begin to prepare the fishballs. First make certain there are no bones in the fish, then puree it together with the other fishball ingredients in a blender or food processor. Dip your fingers in flour and roll the mixture into balls the size of walnuts. Put them on a plate and chill in the refrigerator for at least 15 minutes.

Remove the fish stock from the saucepan and strain into a bowl. Flake the fish and remove any bones or skin. Set aside.

Melt the butter in the saucepan in which you made the fish stock and add the flour. Stir well over low heat for 2 minutes, then gradually add the strained stock, stirring constantly. Add the flaked fish and season to taste with salt and pepper. Do not boil.

Shortly before serving, ladle the fishballs very gently into the soup and poach for 5 minutes. Add the cream and serve.

◪ Mulligatawny Soup

Mulligatawny was such a favorite with the British colonials in India that it quickly became incorporated into the native cuisine back home. The earliest printed recipe for this soup can be found in a cookbook published in 1817. It was written by a young doctor who stated that his purpose was to "make the cage of marriage as comfortable as the net of courtship was charming."

The word "mulligatawny" comes from *milakutanni,* meaning pepper-water. As it is a soup that is both spicy and filling, serve it before something light, such as a Country Fish Pie. *Serves 6.*

2 ounces butter
2 medium-sized onions, chopped
6 cups Chicken Stock
2 tablespoons curry powder
2 cups heavy cream
1 cucumber
1 apple

Melt the butter in a good-sized saucepan. Add the onion and allow it to brown before adding the Chicken Stock and the curry powder.

Bring the mixture to a boil, cover and simmer for 20 minutes.

Strain and allow the soup to cool a little before adding 1 cup of the cream.

Chill in the refrigerator for at least 3 hours.

Before serving, peel the cucumber and apple and dice them into small squares. Add the remaining cup of cream to the soup and sprinkle the cucumber and apple over the top.

◪ Cockie Leekie

Cockie Leekie or Cock-a-Leekie is a traditional Scottish recipe for a very substantial chicken-and-leek soup and is frequently mentioned by Sir Walter Scott in his diaries and books. Cock-fighting was a popular sport in the eighteenth century, and it is believed this soup originated as a way of cooking cocks that had been killed in a cockfight. The addition of prunes may seem strange, but they give the soup a wonderful rich flavor. *Serves 6.*

1 chicken (approximately 3–4 pounds)
11 cups water
6 leeks, washed, trimmed and cut into 1-inch slices
½ cup rice
1 tablespoon salt
1 pound pitted prunes
½ cup chopped parsley

Wash the chicken thoroughly and put it in a large saucepan. Pour in the water and bring to a boil. Add the leeks, rice and salt. Partially cover the saucepan and simmer gently for 2 hours. Add the prunes and continue to simmer for another ½ hour.

Remove the soup from the heat and lift out the chicken. When it is cool enough to handle, remove the skin and cut the meat into thin slices. Return the meat slices to the soup and check to see if the soup needs additional seasoning.

Just before serving, sprinkle with parsley.

◪ Highland Pheasant Soup

Should you just happen to have cooked a pheasant, the next thing to do is to make pheasant soup. However, if you don't have a pheasant on hand, do not be deterred—a turkey carcass will also give you excellent results. Serve with croutons. *Serves 8.*

2 pheasant carcasses and their giblets, or 1 turkey carcass and
* giblets*
2 medium-sized onions, coarsely chopped
1 ounce butter
2 sticks celery, chopped
2 leeks, washed, trimmed and cut into strips
2 carrots, chopped in 1-inch cubes
1 bayleaf
3 parsley sprigs
1 teaspoon salt
4 peppercorns
1 cup sherry

Brown the bones in a pan in the oven for 15 minutes.

Sauté the onions in the butter in a large saucepan until they are well browned and add the bones, giblets, celery, leeks, carrots, bayleaf, parsley, salt and peppercorns. Add enough water to cover the bones and vegetables. Bring the mixture to a boil, cover and simmer for 4 hours without stirring.

Remove from the heat and strain the soup; cool, then skim off the fat.

Reheat, add the sherry and correct the seasoning if necessary.

▧ Brown Windsor Soup

This hearty beef soup, once extremely fashionable, has all but disappeared. For many years, a particularly unappetizing version was continually served by British Railways in their dining cars, which may explain its present demise. Throughout my childhood, I assumed that it was the only soup that could be served on a train, and having tasted it once I knew better than to risk the experience ever again. However, homemade Brown Windsor Soup is altogether different—tasty, nourishing and a meal in itself. *Serves 8.*

2 ounces butter
1 pound stewing beef, cut into cubes
3 medium-sized onions, finely chopped
3 carrots, thinly diced
4 tablespoons flour
10 cups Meat Stock
½ teaspoon thyme
½ teaspoon tarragon
1 bayleaf
Salt
Freshly ground black pepper
1 cup Madeira

Melt the butter in a large, heavy saucepan. Add the meat and vegetables and sauté until lightly browned. Sprinkle on the flour and cook briefly until it has browned. Gradually pour in the stock, stirring constantly. Add the herbs and bayleaf, bring to a boil, cover and simmer for 2 hours.

Season to taste with salt and pepper. Put the soup through a blender or food processor. Reheat, add the Madeira and check the seasoning before serving.

◩ Scotch Broth

Serves 6.

1½ pounds stewing beef or neck of lamb, cut into pieces
8 cups water
3 tablespoons barley
4 carrots, coarsely chopped
3 turnips, coarsely chopped
2 leeks, washed, trimmed and coarsely chopped
1 medium-sized onion, finely chopped
1 cup cabbage, finely chopped
Salt
Freshly ground black pepper
1 tablespoon chopped parsley

Trim any fat off the meat and put it in a large saucepan. Cover with water and bring to a boil. Skim off the top, add the barley and allow to simmer for 1 hour. Add carrots, turnips, leeks and onions and simmer for an additional hour.

Add the cabbage and season to taste with salt and pepper. If the soup seems too thick, add a little water. Simmer for a further 10 minutes, sprinkle with parsley and serve.

◪ Oxtail Soup

This is a classic English soup, popular in the late nineteenth century but for some reason very much less in evidence today. Oxtails are readily available at any good butcher and are surprisingly cheap. The highly glutinous content of the tail bone makes this a wonderfully tasty and nourishing soup to be recommended for a cold winter's evening. *Serves 4–6.*

1 oxtail (approximately 1½ pounds), cut into 2-inch pieces
¼ cup flour
2 ounces butter
1 chopped celery stalk
1 large onion, coarsely chopped
4 carrots, coarsely sliced
10 peppercorns
¼ teaspoon thyme
¼ teaspoon tarragon
1 bayleaf
1 tablespoon salt
5 cups <u>Meat Stock</u>
5 cups water
1 cup sherry or port wine

Coat each piece of oxtail with flour. Melt the butter in a large frying pan and brown both the meat and the vegetables for about 4 minutes.

Transfer to a large saucepan and add the peppercorns, herbs and salt. Add the stock and water. Bring to a boil and skim.

Cover and simmer for 4 hours; remove from heat and strain into a bowl. Take out the meat and when it has cooled separate it from the bones and remove any fatty skin. Return the meat to the soup.

Puree the vegetables in a blender or food processor and return them to the soup.

Transfer the soup to a clean saucepan. Heat to just below the boiling point and add the sherry or port. Adjust the seasoning to taste and serve.

◪ Diana's Lamb Soup

This soup provides the ideal solution for what to do with a leftover lamb bone. It is a meal in itself and can be a comforting antidote to a difficult day. *Serves 6.*

1 good-sized leftover lamb bone (a leg is excellent)
2 ounces butter
1 large onion, chopped
5 cups canned tomatoes in puree
6 cups water
1 tablespoon farina
Salt
Freshly ground black pepper

Remove any fat from the lamb bone. Melt the butter in a large saucepan, add the onions and cook gently until golden. Add the bone, tomatoes, water and farina. Bring to a boil, skim and simmer covered for 5 hours.

Remove the bone. Let the soup cool and put it in the refrigerator. As soon as the fat has congealed, skim it off the top with a spoon. Reheat the soup, add salt and pepper to taste, and serve.

▨ Cold Pease Soup

This traditional English soup ensures a spectacular prelude to any meal. If small, fresh peas are out of season, you may substitute frozen peas. The secret to the taste, however, is the fresh mint, for which there is no substitute. *Serves 6.*

1 pound fresh peas, or one 10-ounce package frozen peas
4 cups Chicken Stock
2 medium-sized onions, chopped
2 crushed garlic cloves
1 ounce butter
2 tablespoons flour
½ small Boston lettuce, shredded
¾ cup fresh mint, finely chopped
2 cups light cream
Salt
Freshly ground black pepper

Cook the peas in the Chicken Stock until they are tender. Using another saucepan, sauté the onion and garlic in the butter until they are a golden color. Add the flour and gradually pour in the Chicken Stock and peas, stirring constantly. Add the lettuce, together with ¼ cup of the mint.

Simmer for 10 minutes, remove from the heat and allow the soup to cool slightly. Puree in a blender or food processor, making sure that you do not overpuree as this should be a coarse-textured soup.

Add the cream. If the soup seems too thick, add a little milk.

Check the seasoning and add salt and pepper to taste.

Allow the soup to chill for several hours and garnish with the remaining mint immediately before serving.

▣ Tomato Soup

The Spanish brought the tomato to Spain from Peru at the end of the sixteenth century and from there it made its way to Italy and France before finally arriving in England. Amazingly enough, it was another hundred years before its culinary potential was discovered, and even then many people still considered it to be poisonous. It was also too expensive to be generally popular.

Perhaps because canned tomato soup is so unspeakably dreary, many people never think about making their own tomato soup. However, it is very simple to prepare and makes the perfect beginning to a summer dinner. *Serves 6.*

2 ounces butter
2 carrots, chopped
2 medium-sized onions, chopped
1 large garlic clove, chopped
6 medium-sized tomatoes, skinned and halved
4 cups Chicken Stock
Salt
Freshly ground black pepper
½ teaspoon nutmeg
Sugar
Juice of half an orange
1 cup heavy cream
3 tablespoons fresh chopped mint

Melt the butter in a large saucepan over low heat. Add the carrots, onion and garlic and cook for approximately 10 minutes. Be careful not to let the vegetables burn.

Add the tomatoes and the stock and continue to cook until the carrots are tender.

Puree the soup in a blender or food processor and season to taste with salt and pepper. Add the nutmeg and a pinch of sugar and pour in the orange juice and cream. If you find the soup is too thick, add a little milk.

Serve either hot or chilled. (If you are serving the soup cold, allow it to chill for at least 2 hours.) Sprinkle the mint on the soup just before serving.

▨ Orange Carrot Soup

Often to be found on an English menu as Crécy Soup, this recipe is easy to prepare and equally good hot or chilled. *Serves 6.*

1 ounce butter
1 pound carrots, peeled and cut into 2-inch slices
3 medium-sized onions, coarsely chopped
2 chopped garlic cloves
⅓ cup flour
6 cups Chicken Stock
1 teaspoon sugar
Juice of one orange
1 cup heavy cream
Salt
Freshly ground black pepper
1 cup chopped watercress

Melt the butter in a large, heavy-bottomed saucepan and add the carrots, onions and garlic. Sauté for about 5 minutes and add the flour. Stir well and gradually add the stock. Bring to a boil and simmer covered for 20 minutes. Add the sugar and continue to simmer for a further 10 minutes.

Remove from the stove and puree in a blender or food processor.

Return the soup to the saucepan and add the orange juice and cream. Season to taste with salt and pepper. If you are serving the soup hot, reheat it very gently, taking care that it does not boil. If you plan to serve it chilled, transfer it to a clean bowl and chill for at least 3 hours.

Garnish with the chopped watercress immediately before serving.

◪ Hampshire Cream Soup

The banks of the River Test in Hampshire are famous for their abundant watercress, which is used in many local dishes. As its name suggests, this soup has a velvety texture and is a delicate pale green color. *Serves 6.*

1 pound carrots, sliced into ¼-inch rounds
1 bunch chopped watercress
2 medium-sized potatoes, peeled and diced
2 large onions, chopped
4–5 cups Chicken Stock
1 cup heavy cream
1 cup sweet sherry
Salt
Freshly ground black pepper

Put the carrots in a good-sized saucepan with the watercress. Add the potatoes, onions and Chicken Stock. Cover and cook over moderate heat until the vegetables are tender.

Remove from the heat and puree in a food processor or blender. Return the pureed soup to the saucepan. Add the cream and sherry, and salt and pepper to taste. If the soup is too thick, add a little milk. Garnish with sprigs of watercress. Serve either hot or chilled.

▣ Saxe-Coburg Soup

The base of this soup is Brussels sprouts, and it was so named in honor of Prince Albert, who came from Saxe-Coburg and was very partial to the vegetable. It is a very good soup and has a way of fooling even those who profess to despise Brussels sprouts. Incidentally, unless you can find very small fresh sprouts, I suggest that you use frozen ones; they work extremely well and are much less trouble to prepare. *Serves 6.*

1 ounce butter
1 medium-sized onion, finely chopped
2 medium-sized potatoes, peeled and diced
4 cups Chicken Stock
1 tablespoon sugar
1 pound Brussels sprouts or one 10-ounce package frozen
  Brussels sprouts
1½ cups light cream
2 ounces cooked ham, finely diced
½ cup sherry
Salt
Freshly ground black pepper

Melt the butter in a good-sized saucepan. Add the onion and sauté gently until the onion is soft but not brown. Add the potatoes, stock, sugar and Brussels sprouts. (If you are using fresh Brussels sprouts, trim the stalks and remove the outer leaves before adding them to the soup.)

Bring the soup to a boil, lower the heat, cover and simmer for about 15 minutes or until the sprouts and potatoes are tender.

Remove the soup and puree it in a blender or food processor before returning it to the same saucepan. Stir in the cream, ham and sherry and season to taste with salt and pepper.

If you are serving the soup hot, heat it gently but do not let it boil. If you plan to serve it cold, chill it in the refrigerator for several hours before serving.

◪ Turnip Soup

What could be more English than turnip soup? Both Mrs. Acton and Mrs. Beeton, those two great ladies of English cooking, offer their readers very similar recipes although Mrs. Beeton names her recipe "Prince of Wales Soup" and claims it was invented by a philanthropic friend to be distributed among the poor on the Prince of Wales's eighteenth birthday.

Apart from substituting Chicken Stock for veal stock and reducing the quantities, this recipe follows very closely the directions given by Mesdames Acton and Beeton. *Serves 4–6.*

1½ pounds turnips, peeled and sliced
2 large onions, chopped
6 cups Chicken Stock
½ teaspoon sugar
Salt
Freshly ground black pepper
1 cup heavy cream
1 cup milk

Put the turnips, onions and Chicken Stock in a large saucepan and cook gently for about 20 minutes or until the vegetables are soft and tender.

Puree the mixture in a blender or food processor and return the soup to the same saucepan. Add the sugar and season to taste with salt and pepper.

Reheat the soup and add the cream and milk just before serving. If the soup seems too thick, add a few more tablespoons of milk.

▨ Cawl Mamgu

The leek is the national emblem of Wales, and on Saint David's Day the Welsh traditionally wear leek leaves pinned to their clothes. (Saint David is the patron saint of Wales.) Leeks are an ingredient in many Welsh dishes and Cawl Mamgu (*cawl* means broth and is pronounced cowl) is a very ancient Welsh recipe for leek soup. *Serves 4–6.*

4 medium-sized leeks, washed, trimmed and cut into small cubes
2 large onions, peeled
3 carrots, peeled and sliced in small cubes
2 parsnips, peeled and sliced in small cubes
1½ pounds neck of lamb, sliced and trimmed of any fat
½ cup rice
Salt
Freshly ground black pepper
1 bunch of parsley, finely chopped

Make a bunch of the well-washed leaves of one of the leeks, the parsley stalks and the onion skins. Wrap them in cheesecloth and secure with string at either end.

Put the vegetables in a large saucepan with the meat, rice and the bunch of flavoring leaves. Add a little salt and pepper and cover with cold water. Bring the mixture slowly to a boil, skim it once or twice, then cover and simmer over low heat for 2 hours.

Remove the meat bones and the bunch of skins. Check the seasoning. Sprinkle the parsley on top just before serving.

⊠ Winter Vegetable Soup

This is a wonderfully thick, creamy soup that is both filling and elegant. Served with bread, cheese and a salad, it makes a complete meal. *Serves 6.*

1 chopped carrot
5 medium-sized potatoes, peeled and cut into large cubes
5 medium-sized onions, coarsely chopped
2 leeks, washed, trimmed and coarsely chopped
1 stick of frozen butter
1 tablespoon salt
Freshly ground black pepper
5 tomatoes, skinned and quartered (preferably fresh)
½ pound mushrooms, cut lengthwise
1 cup cream
1 bunch of watercress, chopped

Place the carrot, potatoes, onions and leeks in a large saucepan. Cover them with water and add the butter, salt and a generous amount of pepper.

Bring the water to a boil, cover the saucepan and simmer for 25 minutes. Remove from heat and puree about ⅔ of the soup in a food processor or blender. Return the pureed soup to the saucepan and mix it in with the unpureed soup. Add the tomatoes and mushrooms and simmer for another 10 minutes.

Before serving, add the cream and watercress. If necessary, reheat the soup, but do not allow it to boil.

Fish

Kipper Pâté
Potted Shrimps
Shrimp Paste
Fish and Chips
Soused Mackerel
Grilled Mackerel
Trout Fried in Oatmeal
Mussel Pie
Country Fish Pie
Soles in Their Coffins
Tweed Kettle
Haddock Savoy
Fried Eel and Parsley

OTHER FISH RECIPES INCLUDED
IN THE BREAKFAST SECTION:

Kedgeree
Fishcakes
Creamed Finnan Haddie

The phrase came to be synonymous with "muddle" or "mess," but only because British waters abound in such a variety of fish that a good catch might contain an almost undecipherable variety: brill, cod, whiting, halibut, turbot, sole, flounder, haddock, carp, plaice, trout, mackerel, perch, whitebait, prawns, shrimps and herring.

London's hawkers used to shout their "oysters, three pence a peck," "new greate cockles," "lilywhite mussels," "new plaice, mackerel" and "new haddocks new." Fish-and-chips shops are still an institution in virtually every town, the last remaining legacy of the food stalls that became popular at the end of the eighteenth century. Set up to provide quick and nourishing hot food for factory workers, they did a busy trade in fish, pies, cockles, mussels and eels.

However, much of the seafood, that was then cheap and plentiful, such as salmon, oysters, crabs and lobsters, has now become scarce and expensive. Oysters were once so common that they were used as a sausage filling in place of more expensive meat, and salmon was among the few fish the poor in Scotland could afford. Lampreys (Henry I ate so many of them one day that he literally died of indigestion) and sturgeon (so valued that only the king was allowed to eat it) have almost died out.

The Victorians ate a lot of fish and since Britain is a small island, there was always a great quantity of fresh fish available. In fact, most markets were in such daily contact with ocean fishing that Mrs. Beeton had to warn her readers that even "a few hours of bad weather at sea" could raise the price of a turbot twentyfold.

Sadly, the twentieth-century scourge of frozen fish has put many an English fishmonger out of business and has made it much harder to find some of the lesser-known varieties of English fish. However, if you are visiting Britain, ask and with luck you may even be able to find such regional dishes as Star Gazey Pie (so called because the pilchards in it are arranged so that their heads peep out of the pastry and look up to heaven), Glasgow Magistrates (made from Loch Fyne herrings, which are so plump they resemble courtroom officials) and Pastai Gocos (a traditional Welsh cockle pie).

▨ Kipper Pâté

This makes an excellent first course or can be served as a dip. It is both simple and quick to prepare. If you are unable to find fresh kippers, substitute a can of kipper fillets. Another alternative is to use smoked whitefish. Serve with toast or crackers. *Serves 4–6.*

2 kippers or 1 six-ounce can kipper fillets
6 ounces softened butter
2 tablespoons lemon juice
¼ teaspoon mace
Salt
Freshly ground black pepper

Place the kippers in a shallow dish and pour on enough boiling water to cover them. Let stand for 10 minutes; drain carefully and remove the skin and bones.

Add the softened butter and pound to a paste. This can be done in a blender or food processor. Add the lemon juice and mace and season with salt and pepper.

Place the pâté in a small dish, cover and chill. Allow the pâté to stand at room temperature for at least ½ hour before serving, otherwise it will not be soft enough.

◪ Potted Shrimps

There is nothing that can quite compare with potted Morecambe Bay shrimps. Famous the world over, these tiny, tasty
shrimps, covered with a coating of clarified butter, date from
the time when the thrifty housewives of Morecambe would pot
their extra shrimps as a way to preserve them. Unfortunately
these shrimps are not available in this country. However, you
can come up with a very acceptable substitute if you use fresh
shrimps and cut them into small pieces or use the bottled baby
shrimps that can be found in most good delicatessens. Serve
with buttered brown bread as a first course. *Serves 4.*

8 ounces unsalted butter
10 ounces shrimps, cooked and peeled (see note above)
2 teaspoons lemon juice
Salt
Freshly ground black pepper
½ teaspoon nutmeg

Melt 3 ounces of the butter in a heavy saucepan over very low
heat. As soon as it has melted, remove it from the heat and stir
in the shrimps, lemon juice, salt and pepper to taste, and the
nutmeg. Mix well and place the mixture in 4 individual soufflé
dishes or small pots. Allow to cool.

Melt the remaining butter in a heavy saucepan over low heat.
When it has melted, skim the foam off the top and spoon out
the clear butter, leaving any sediment that has collected at the
bottom.

Pour the clear (clarified) butter over the shrimps and chill them
in the refrigerator for at least 6 hours.

◙ Shrimp Paste

½ pound shrimps, cooked and peeled
5 tablespoons olive oil
Juice of a lime
¼ teaspoon Cayenne pepper
½ teaspoon dried basil
¼ teaspoon ground coriander seeds
Salt

Mash the shrimps to a paste. This can be done either by using a fork or in a blender or food processor. Gradually add the olive oil. Season with the lime juice, cayenne pepper, basil and coriander. Add salt to taste. Place in a small jar or dish. Cover and refrigerate for several hours. Serve chilled with toast or crackers.

◪ Fish and Chips

The time-honored tradition of fish and chips is still going strong. To be considered truly authentic, the chips should be doused in vinegar, which is much tastier than ketchup. The traditional batter is very simple and contains no eggs or milk. Surprisingly enough, it is far crisper than a more sophisticated batter. *Serves 6.*

1¾ cups flour
1 teaspoon baking soda
Salt
Approximately 1 cup water
2 pounds fresh whitefish fillets such as flounder, cod or haddock
   (if possible they should not be skinned, as the skin
   gives them much of their flavor)
Oil for deep-fat frying
CHIPS:
2 pounds potatoes, peeled and sliced in thin strips

Mix the flour, baking soda and a pinch of salt in a bowl. Make a well in the center and gradually add the water to make a smooth batter. If it is too thick, add a little more water. Allow the batter to stand for 1 hour.

Dry the fish with paper towels and sprinkle each fillet with a little flour and salt.

Heat the oil in a saucepan. Dip the fish in the batter and deep fry them until they are golden brown, about 5 minutes. Drain the cooked fillets and place them on a serving dish. Keep them warm in the oven until you are ready to serve them.

Dry the potatoes, sprinkle them with salt and deep fry them until they are golden brown. Drain and serve with the fish.

⊠ Soused Mackerel

This recipe from Cornwall makes a good summer lunch or supper dish. Cooking the mackerel in vinegar helps to preserve the natural oil content of the fish. It is typically served with <u>Spiced Cabbage</u>. *Serves 6.*

6 mackerel, cleaned
2 medium-sized onions, finely chopped
1 tablespoon chopped parsley
3 bayleaves
8 cloves
⅛ teaspoon mace
Sprig of thyme or ¼ teaspoon thyme leaves
6 peppercorns
Salt
2 cups tarragon vinegar

Preheat the oven to 350°.

Place the mackerel in an ovenproof baking dish and cover with the onions, parsley, bayleaves, cloves, mace, thyme, peppercorns and a sprinkling of salt.

Pour the vinegar over the mackerel and bake for 30 minutes. Remove from the oven and allow to cool slightly.

Lift out the mackerel very carefully and arrange in a good-sized serving dish that has a rim at least 1 inch high. Strain the cooking liquid and pour it over the fish.

Refrigerate and allow to souse or marinate for several hours before serving. The liquid will form a tasty aspic jelly around the fish.

◪ Grilled Mackerel

I was once told that until the eighteenth century, mackerel was the only fish that could legally be sold on Sundays. I have never been able to verify this fact but perhaps it explains why mackerel has always been such a popular fish in England. In Cornwall, it is traditional to serve Gooseberry Sauce with mackerel—strange but delicious. *Serves 4.*

4 mackerel, cleaned and with their heads removed
2 tablespoons flour
2 ounces butter
Sprig of fennel
½ cup chopped parsley
1 lemon, cut into quarters

Split the fish open down their bellies so that they lie flat. Dust them generously with flour and sauté them in butter with fennel for approximately 4 minutes.

Remove from the pan and arrange on a serving dish. Sprinkle with parsley and garnish with the lemon quarters. Serve immediately.

▣ Trout Fried in Oatmeal

In Scotland you might very well get this for breakfast. I suggest, however, that you try it for lunch or supper, accompanied by Mustard Sauce. The oatmeal makes an exceptionally light, crisp batter. *Serves 6.*

6 trout, cleaned
Salt
2 beaten eggs
Freshly ground black pepper
1 cup oatmeal
2 ounces lard
1½ ounces butter
2 lemons, cut in round slices
5 sprigs parsley

Wash the trout, wipe dry and sprinkle the insides with salt. Dip each one in the egg and coat thickly with oatmeal, which should first be seasoned with a little salt and pepper.

Melt the lard in a frying pan and fry the trout for 3 minutes on each side. Place the fish on a paper towel to remove any excess fat, then transfer to a warm serving dish.

Place a little butter on top of each dish and decorate with the lemon slices and parsley.

◪ Mussel Pie

A rather unexpected way to cook mussels that is quite good. *Serves 4–6.*

2 quarts mussels (about 45 mussels)
1 cup white wine
5 sprigs parsley
2 small onions, finely chopped
1 tablespoon chopped parsley
Freshly ground black pepper
Salt
3 cups stale white breadcrumbs
1½ ounces butter

Wash and scrub the mussels and remove their beards. Place them in a large kettle with the wine and the parsley sprigs. Cover tightly and boil for about 4 minutes, shaking the kettle from time to time, until the mussels have opened.

Remove the mussels and take them out of their shells, holding them over the kettle so as not to lose any of the liquid. Strain all the cooking liquor from the kettle into a bowl.

Put the mussels in a shallow ovenproof dish and pour over them ½ cup of the strained liquor. Sprinkle the onions and chopped parsley over the mussels and add a generous amount of salt and pepper. Cover with breadcrumbs and add a little more of the strained liquor so that the breadcrumbs are damp but not swimming. Dot with butter and bake for 20 minutes at 350°. Then place for a few minutes under the broiler to brown.

◩ Country Fish Pie

Fish pie is simple, unpretentious and extremely good. Serve it with a green salad. *Serves 4–6.*

1 pound whitefish fillets (flounder, cod, whiting or perch)
2 cups milk
Salt
Freshly ground black pepper
4 ounces butter
⅓ cup flour
1½ cups mushrooms, sliced lengthwise
3 medium-sized tomatoes, peeled and quartered
8 ounces peeled shrimps
1 tablespoon lemon juice
2 tablespoons sour cream
4 medium-sized potatoes, boiled and mashed with lots of
*   butter and a little milk*

Preheat the oven to 350°.

Put the fish in a baking pan with the milk and a sprinkling of salt and pepper. Bake in the oven for 10–15 minutes until the fillets are cooked. The time will vary slightly, depending on what fish you choose and the thickness of the fillets.

Remove the fish from the oven and flake it into small pieces. Be sure to take out any bones. Strain the milk in which the fish was cooked into a small bowl.

Melt 2 ounces of the butter in a pan. Stir in the flour and cook for about 2 minutes, stirring constantly. Gradually add the fish liquor and cook over low heat, still stirring constantly, until you have a creamy sauce.

Sauté the mushrooms, tomatoes and shrimps in 1 ounce of the butter for a few minutes. Add them to the sauce together with the lemon and sour cream. Season to taste with salt and pepper.

Put the fish in an ovenproof baking dish and pour the sauce on top. Cover this with mashed potato. Do not try to smooth down the potato; leave it bumpy and dot the remaining butter on top.

Bake for 20 minutes. Then place the dish under the broiler for a few minutes so that it can brown. Serve immediately.

▨ Soles in Their Coffins

This Victorian recipe is fairly elaborate but worth the trouble to prepare not only for its amusing name but also for its looks and taste. *Serves 4.*

8 small fillets of sole
2 cups white wine
1 small onion, finely chopped
Salt
Freshly ground black pepper
2 ounces butter
⅓ cup flour
4 large potatoes, baked in their jackets
1 cup mushrooms, cut lengthwise
4 ounces peeled shrimps
Butter
Milk
4–5 sprigs of parsley

Preheat the oven to 350°

Roll the fillets and put them in an ovenproof dish with the wine and chopped onion. Sprinkle with salt and pepper, cover and bake for about 8 minutes—depending on the thickness of the fillets. Be sure not to overcook.

Remove the fillets very carefully from the pan and set aside. Strain the liquid into a small bowl.

Melt the butter in a saucepan. Add the flour and stir for 2 minutes. Gradually add the strained cooking liquid to make a creamy sauce and remove from the heat.

Cut a slice from the long side of each potato and scoop out the potato inside very carefully. Set aside.

Sauté the mushrooms and shrimps in a little butter for a few minutes.

Pour a little sauce into each potato. Put 2 fish fillets on top of the sauce, add the shrimps and mushrooms and replace the caps on the potatoes.

Put the stuffed potatoes on a baking pan and heat for 10 minutes at 400°. At the same time mash the scooped-out potato with butter and milk and plenty of salt and pepper.

Place the stuffed potatoes on a large serving dish and arrange the mashed potatoes in small mounds around the coffins. Garnish with parsley and serve.

◙ Tweed Kettle

A delicious salmon stew from Scotland. If you happen to have a leftover piece of salmon tail this is what you should do with it. *Serves 4.*

1½ pounds salmon
Salt
Pepper
¼ teaspoon mace
2½ cups white wine
1½ teaspoons chopped chives
2 ounces softened butter
1 tablespoon parsley

Simmer the salmon for 5 minutes in boiling water. Drain it and remove the skin and bones.

Cut the salmon flesh into 2-inch pieces and season with a little salt and pepper and the mace. Place the fish in an ovenproof pan with the wine and chives and simmer uncovered for 5 minutes.

Lift out the salmon pieces and place them on a serving dish. Reduce the cooking liquid to approximately ¾ cup. Stir in the butter and pour the mixture over the salmon. Garnish with parsley and serve.

▨ Haddock Savoy

This recipe for haddock served in a delicate cheese sauce was created in the kitchens of the Savoy Hotel at the end of the nineteenth century. *Serves 4.*

1½ pounds cooked smoked haddock
¼ cup Parmesan cheese
Salt
Cayenne pepper
2 eggs
2 cups heavy cream

Preheat the oven to 300°.

Flake the fish and remove any skin and bones. Mix it with the cheese and a little salt and pepper.

Beat the eggs.

Bring the cream to a boil and pour it over the eggs, stirring constantly.

Pour the sauce over the fish and spoon the mixture into a buttered ovenproof dish. Put the dish in a pan of warm water and bake for 20 minutes.

◙ Fried Eel and Parsley

Eels have always been found in abundant quantity in British rivers and estuaries. They come there to spawn from the Sargasso Sea in the Atlantic. Eel and pie shops, where one could buy jellied or stewed eels and meat pies, used to flourish in every British town, but have now completely disappeared, having been superseded at the beginning of this century by the fish-and-chips shop. *Serves 6.*

2 tablespoons flour
½ teaspoon salt
½ teaspoon freshly ground black pepper
2 pounds eel, cleaned, skinned and cut into 3-inch pieces
6 ounces butter
Juice of 1 lemon
10 sprigs parsley
Oil for frying

Mix the flour with salt and pepper and roll the pieces of eel in it.

Fry the eel in half of the butter until it is golden brown and the flesh begins to come away from the bones.

Melt the remaining butter, mix it with the lemon juice and pour it in a pitcher. Stand the pitcher in a bowl of hot water.

Fry the parsley in a little oil and wrap it around the eel pieces. Transfer them to a serving dish, pour the sauce over them and serve.

Meat,
Poultry
and
Game

Roast Beef and Yorkshire Pudding
Steak and Kidney Pudding
Steak and Kidney Pie
Beef Wellington
Scotch Collops
Beef Guinness
Shepherd's Pie
Boiled Beef with Carrots and Dumplings
Chiddingly Hot Pot
Guard of Honor with Herb Pudding
Reform Cutlets
Lancashire Hot Pot
Irish Stew
Oxtail Stew
Curate's Cheek
Penny's Pork with Chestnuts
Marbled Veal
Veal, Ham and Egg Pie
Melton Mowbray Pork Pie
Hindle Wakes
Stoved Chicken
Coronation Chicken
Roast Chicken with Cranberry Stuffing
Fried Chicken with Gubbins Sauce
Miss McFarlane's Honey-Glazed Chicken
Roast Goose with Sage and Onion Stuffing
Roast Pheasant
Dorothy Ballam's Poacher's Pie
Mixed Grill
Skuets

I wyll roste my pygges or ever I spytte my capons.
—John Palsgrave, 1530

Foreigners may not always appreciate British cooking, but they grudgingly admit the British have a right to be respected for the abundance and quality of their meat in general and their beef in particular.

The British have always been prodigious meat eaters, and it is no accident that John Bull, that obese gentleman with a bull-dog snapping at his heels and his face flushed from a diet of beef and ale, became the symbol and personification of England. Up to the eighteenth century, however, English cattle were as small and tough as their European counterparts and there was nothing particularly distinguished about English roast beef. All of this changed thanks to the efforts of two men: Lord Townshend and Robert Bakewell.

Townshend, known as "Turnip Townshend," came up with the revolutionary idea of feeding cattle and pigs on turnips during the winter months instead of slaughtering them. This led Robert Bakewell, who was still in his teens when Townshend died in 1738, to realize that improved livestock was the key to successful farming. He conducted numerous stock-breeding experiments that soon resulted in a radical improvement in the quality of beef cattle. The culmination of his experiments was the creation of the Aberdeen Angus, which even today is considered the best of all beef cattle herds. Within a short time, Britain was established as the major stock breeder of the world and her beef was the envy of every nation.

There is no doubt that Roast Beef and Yorkshire Pudding is the national dish of England. The beef is always called "a joint," and traditionally it is eaten at Sunday dinner, which is called lunch and served in the middle of the day. In the eighteenth and nineteenth centuries Sunday joints were huge, averaging about twenty-four pounds, and a piece of meat weighing only ten pounds was referred to as a Tom Thumb joint.

Nowadays, we are warned about the dangers of eating too much meat. But in 1817, Dr. Kitchiner, writing in *The Cook's Oracle of Health,* advised his readers never to eat less than six pounds of meat a week! Meat was plentiful and cheap and even the less well-to-do were accustomed to eating large amounts. However, fuel was scarce and expensive and since most people did not have large fireplaces in their homes, it was the custom to stop by the baker on the way to church on Sunday morning and cook one's joint in his oven, since no bread was baked on Sundays.

Meat left over from the Sunday joint would appear in a variety of ways throughout the rest of the week and this gave rise to the old ditty:

Hot on Sunday,
Cold on Monday,
Hashed on Tuesday,
Minced on Wednesday,
Curried on Thursday,
Broth on Friday,
Cottage pie Saturday.

But there is more to British meat than beef. What could be more British than lamb or mutton? In the United States as well as in England, lamb is plentiful, although often frozen, and real mutton is almost unobtainable. This is a recent phenomenon, however, and one that is due to the development of refrigeration. Victorian cookery books give three times as many recipes for mutton as for lamb, indicating how quickly, as spring became summer, lamb in the shops turned to mutton. Perhaps we can thank those unlucky cooks who were trying to pass off their "mutton dressed as lamb" for the invention of that great English institution—Mint Sauce, without which no self-respecting Briton would now presume to eat even lamb, let alone mutton.

Also not to be overlooked is the great tradition of English meat pies: Pork Pie, Veal and Ham Pie, Steak and Kidney Pie, Shepherd's Pie, et al. Many of these date from medieval times, when they were known as raised or coffin pies because of their shape.

Britain is also famous for her game and poultry. Geese, ducks, partridge, pheasant, grouse, snipe, woodcock, swans, wild boar and peacocks all used to be eaten in great quantity, but today most game is scarce and expensive. Prized above all else is the red grouse, which can be found only on the moors in the north of England and Scotland.

Grouse shooting is a serious business. The season begins on the "Glorious Twelfth" of August, unless this date happens to fall on a Sunday, in which case the birds are given an extra day's grace. It stretches until December 10 and is as important a part of the social scene as Wimbledon or Ascot.

Each year the race to bring the first birds to the tables of the top hotels and restaurants of London is fast and furious. Bagging a brace (catching two grouse) is no small undertaking. It involves Land Rovers, retrievers, gamekeepers, beaters and a good pair of twelve-gauge double-barreled sidelock ejector guns, which can cost up to $22,000. The correct outfit is knicker-bockers, heavy woolen socks, special gum boots and a tweed cap. This ritualistic, expensive enterprise still attracts sportsmen from all over the world. To those who like it, there is no greater delicacy than grouse. But not everyone feels this way:

> Housewarming at Zola's. . . . very tasty dinner . . . including some grouse whose scented flesh Daudet compared to an old courtesan's flesh marinated in a bidet.
>
> *—Edmond de Goncourt, 1878*

Even today the British diet is extremely carnivorous, and the recipes included in this chapter attempt to give a sense of the variety of roasts, stews and pies that are so much a part of the traditional British table.

◩ Roast Beef and Yorkshire Pudding

It used to be the custom to cook the Yorkshire Pudding around the Roast Beef in the same pan. Although this is rarely done today, Yorkshire Pudding still tastes best if it is cooked in the fat that the meat has been cooked in, so that it absorbs the meat juices. Serve with Horseradish Sauce. *Serves 6.*

4 pounds rib roast
2 tablespoons oil
YORKSHIRE PUDDING:
¾ cup flour
½ teaspoon salt
¾ cup milk
1 tablespoon water
2 eggs

Preheat the oven to 450°.

Place the beef fat side up in a roasting pan and coat it with the oil.

If you like your beef rare, it should cook for 1¼ hours and a meat thermometer should register between 130° and 140°. If you prefer it medium to well done, it should cook for 1½ hours and a meat thermometer should register between 150° and 160°. Baste the meat frequently while it is cooking.

Meanwhile, prepare the batter for the Yorkshire pudding: Sift the flour and salt into a mixing bowl. Make a well in the center and add the milk and the water gradually, beating with a wooden spoon.

In a separate bowl, beat the eggs until fluffy. Add them to the flour mixture. Beat until bubbles rise to the surface. Pour the batter into a pitcher and refrigerate it for ½ hour.

When the meat is cooked, remove it from the pan and place it on a warm platter. Cover with aluminum foil and let stand for 25 minutes before carving.

Rebeat the batter and pour it quickly into the still-hot cooking pan. Bake it in the oven for 10 minutes at 450°. Then reduce the heat to 350° and cook it for an additional 15 minutes, until it is well risen and has turned a golden brown. (Do not open the oven door while it is cooking.) Serve immediately from the pan in which it has been cooked.

◪ Steak and Kidney Pudding

This most British of all puddings looks unlike anything else and tastes remarkably good. The traditional method of preparing it is to place the raw meat in a pudding bowl, cover it with pastry and steam for 4 hours. The length of cooking time tends to make the pastry somewhat soggy and heavy. For this reason, I prefer to cook the meat ahead of time and steam the pudding for a much shorter period. This method has the added advantage of allowing you to prepare the meat in advance. It can even be done the day before if this is more convenient.

Traditionally, a steak and kidney pudding is served directly from the dish in which it has been cooked, which is wrapped around with a clean cloth or white napkin, and accompanied by Brussels sprouts and new potatoes. *Serves 6.*

1 large onion, coarsely chopped
3 ounces butter
1¼ pounds lean chuck beef, cut into 1-inch cubes
½ pound veal kidneys, cut into ½-inch pieces
⅓ cup flour, seasoned with salt and pepper
1½ cups mushrooms, cut into quarters
1 tablespoon parsley
1 bayleaf
Salt
Freshly ground black pepper
1 tablespoon Worcestershire sauce
1½ cups <u>Meat Stock</u>
2 tablespoons tomato puree
SUET PASTRY:
2 cups flour
2 teaspoons baking powder
1 cup shredded suet
Salt
Freshly ground black pepper
6 tablespoons water

Fry the onion in the butter until it is browned. Set aside.

Remove any fat or gristle from the steak and kidneys and toss them in the seasoned flour. Sauté lightly in the butter and transfer to a casserole. Fry the mushrooms for 2 minutes and add them and the onion to the meats. Add the parsley, bayleaf and a generous sprinkling of salt and pepper.

Mix the stock with the Worcestershire sauce and tomato puree and pour it over the meat. Cover and simmer in a 300° oven for one hour or until the meat is just tender.

Remove and allow to cool. If the gravy is too thin, reduce it by boiling over a high heat until it has thickened.

TO PREPARE THE PASTRY: Combine the flour, baking powder and suet in a bowl. Add a generous pinch of salt and a little pepper. When the mixture has the consistency of coarse breadcrumbs, make a well in the center and add 6 tablespoons cold water. Mix to a soft dough, kneading as little as possible. If the dough is too crumbly, add a little more water, but don't overdo it as the dough should be on the dry side.

Form the dough into a ball and place it on a lightly floured surface. Roll out ⅔ of it and use it to line an English pudding bowl or a Pyrex bowl that holds approximately 7 cups. Push the pastry down with your fingers and work it around the sides so that it fits neatly and reaches over the top of the bowl. Do not trim the pastry at this point; allow it to hang over the top. Place the meat in the bowl and roll out the remaining pastry so that it will fit over the top of the bowl. Moisten the edges with water so that it adheres properly and crimp it down with a fork so that it is sealed very tightly. Now trim off any excess pastry and cover the top of the bowl with a loose-fitting foil cover. Make a pleat in it so that there is room for the pastry to rise and tie it tightly around the rim with string. Any steam that gets in will make the pastry soggy.

Place the bowl on a steamer rack or a saucer turned upside down in a large pot of boiling water. The water should reach halfway up the basin. Make sure the water is boiling, then cover the pot tightly and reduce the heat to very low. Steam the pudding for 1½ hours, checking from time to time to be sure that the water holds its level and continues to boil gently. If the water level begins to sink, pour in more.

TO SERVE: Remove the bowl from the saucepan. Take off the foil and sponge off the outside of the bowl. Wrap a clean white cloth or napkin around it and knot it. When you serve the pudding, use a spoon and not a knife to cut into the crust.

◪ Steak and Kidney Pie

Steak and Kidney Pie is a variation of Steak and Kidney Pudding. It uses the identical meat filling, but instead of being steamed in a pudding bowl, it is made with a regular pie crust and baked in the oven. *Serves 6.*

MEAT FILLING:
Use the ingredients given in the recipe for Steak and Kidney Pudding.
SHORTCRUST PASTRY:
2¼ cups flour
¼ teaspoon salt
3 ounces unsalted butter
4 ounces lard
1 tablespoon confectioners' sugar
1 egg yolk
3 tablespoons cold water
Milk and beaten egg to brush pastry with

Prepare the meat filling as in the Steak and Kidney Pudding recipe and allow it to cool.

TO PREPARE THE PASTRY: Sift the flour and salt into a mixing bowl. Cut the butter and lard into small pieces and mix them into the flour with the blade of a knife until they are well coated. Using your fingertips, rub in the fat until the mixture resembles fine breadcrumbs. Stir in the sugar. Mix the egg yolk with the water and pour into the flour. Mix quickly with a palette knife until it forms a dough. Knead the pastry lightly until it is smooth and has no cracks. Wrap it in waxed paper and chill in the refrigerator for 30 minutes.

Preheat the oven to 450°.

Divide the pastry into 2 halves and roll out one half to about ¼-inch thickness. Use it to line a deep 9″ pie dish. Place the meat filling on top of the pastry and roll out the remaining pastry to make a cover.

Brush a little water over the rim of the pastry case before placing the pastry cover over it. Press down the edges with a fork.

(Use any leftover trimmings to make leaves to decorate the top of the pie.)

Make a hole in the center of the pie to let out the steam while it cooks. A pie funnel can be used if you have one. Brush the pastry with a little milk and beaten egg.

Bake at 450° for 20 minutes, then reduce the heat to 325° and continue to cook the pie for a further ½ hour.

◨ Beef Wellington

This recipe is rather a mystery. I have never been able to find a reference to Beef Wellington in any British cookery book, old or new. However, since this method of cooking meat in a pastry case was fairly common at the end of the eighteenth century and since this is a rather special way to prepare a beef fillet, it would seem unfair to omit Beef Wellington for its dubious heritage. Serve with <u>Horseradish Sauce</u> and <u>Braised Parsnips</u>. *Serves 6–8.*

1 ounce butter
2 cups mushrooms, finely chopped
1 medium-sized onion, finely chopped
Salt
Freshly ground black pepper
2 teaspoons chopped parsley
2 eggs, beaten
2-pound fillet of beef
PUFF PASTRY:
2¼ cups flour
Salt
3 ounces lard
5 ounces unsalted butter
¼ teaspoon lemon juice
5–6 tablespoons ice cold water

Melt the butter in a pan over low heat and add the mushrooms and onion. When the onion has turned a golden color, add a little salt and pepper together with the chopped parsley, and allow the mixture to cool. Stir in 1 egg and set aside while you prepare the pastry.

TO PREPARE THE PASTRY: Sift the flour and salt into a large bowl. Cut the lard and butter into small cubes and stir them into the flour with the blade of a knife. Add the lemon juice and 5 tablespoons of water. Keep mixing with the knife blade until you can shape the mixture into a ball. (If you need more liquid, use the extra tablespoon of water.) Place the pastry ball in a plastic bag and chill it in the refrigerator for about 15 minutes.

Preheat the oven to 250°.

Roll out the pastry into an oblong shape about ¼-inch thick and then fold it in thirds, pressing the edges with the side of your hand to seal in the air. Give the pastry a quarter turn and roll it out again (you will be rolling it in the opposite direction), and again fold it in thirds and press down the edges. Repeat this operation of rolling, folding, sealing and turning twice more. If the pastry begins to get sticky, put it back in the refrigerator for 10 minutes.

Cut the pastry into 2 pieces, one of which should be ¾ of its weight. Roll the larger piece on a floured board into a large oval shape. Place it on a well-greased roasting pan and lay the beef in the center.

Spread the mushroom and onion mixture over the top of the meat and roll out the remaining piece of pastry into a long strip. Bring the lower piece of pastry up around the beef. Brush the edges with water and place the other piece of pastry over the top of the meat. Press the edges together and use any trimmings to make leaves to decorate the top.

Brush the pastry with the remaining egg. Prick a few holes in the top and bake for 15 minutes at 250°. Turn down the heat to 200° and bake for a further 15 minutes.

Allow the meat to stand for 15 minutes in a warm place before serving.

▦ Scotch Collops

There are many different collop recipes to be found in old English cookery books. Originally the word meant a slice of meat that came off the animal's back, but now it seems to refer to any cut of meat. Mrs. Beeton has recipes for veal, venison and beef collops. She also includes the following anecdote, which tells something about how the Victorians felt regarding the subject:

> A strong-minded lady was inquiring after the character of a cook she was about to hire. The lady who was giving the character entered a little upon the cook's moral qualifications and described her as a very decent woman, to which [came] the astounding reply . . . "Oh d'n her decency; can she make good collops?"

Serves 4.

2 ounces butter
1 tablespoon oil
4 medium-sized onions, finely chopped
4 slices thin rump steak (about 6 ounces each)
Salt
Freshly ground black pepper
2 cups mushrooms, finely sliced

Heat the butter and oil in a frying pan and sauté the onions until they are golden brown. Remove from the heat and set aside.

Brown the steaks for 2 minutes on either side and place on top of the onions in a warmed serving dish. Season with salt and pepper.

Sauté the mushrooms in the frying pan for 3 minutes and add salt and pepper. Spoon them over the steak and serve.

▨ Beef Guinness

This is a rich, tasty, brown stew that is cooked in Guinness—a popular British ale, available in most American supermarkets and liquor stores. Serve this stew with new potatoes. *Serves 6.*

3 tablespoons oil
Salt
2 pounds chuck steak, sliced approximately 2–3 inches long and
  ½-inch thick
7 medium-sized onions, coarsely chopped
Freshly ground black pepper
2 tablespoons flour
½ can beef consommé
1 bottle Guinness (6½ fluid ounces)
3 tablespoons brown sugar
2 tablespoons vinegar

Preheat the oven to 250°.

Place 2 tablespoons of oil and the salt in a frying pan and brown the meat in it. Transfer the meat to a large ovenproof casserole and, using the same frying pan, salt and brown the onions and add them to the meat in the casserole. Season with pepper and set aside.

In the frying pan, make a roux with the flour and the remaining tablespoon of oil. Add the consommé and stir until the mixture is smooth and there are no lumps in it. Add to the casserole. Mix the Guinness with the brown sugar and vinegar and pour over the meat. Cover the casserole and cook in a 250° oven for 2½ hours.

◻ Shepherd's Pie

The Eastbourne Board of Guardians have ordered a
mincing machine . . . for the use of aged and toothless
paupers in their workhouse.
—Pall Mall Gazette, 1885

Shepherd's Pie has always been a favorite standby for institutional cooks and has been forced unwillingly on successive generations of schoolchildren, prison inmates and paying guests in seaside establishments of dubious quality. Traditionally, an authentic Shepherd's Pie is made with leftover roast lamb that has been put through a mincer. However, it is much easier to make it from fresh ground lamb or ground beef, and despite its poor reputation it is not only an excellent way to feed a large number of people, but an effective dish to serve just a few! *Serves 6.*

3 tablespoons oil
2 medium-sized onions, finely chopped
2 garlic cloves, finely chopped
1½ pounds ground lamb or ground beef
1 6-ounce can tomato paste
2 bouillon cubes
1 heaped tablespoon flour
1 cup white wine
½ cup water
Salt
Freshly ground black pepper
½ teaspoon tarragon
3 large potatoes, peeled
3 ounces butter
1 cup milk
½ cup cooked corn
2 tablespoons Parmesan cheese

Preheat the oven to 350°.

Heat the oil in a large frying pan over low heat. Add the onion and garlic and cook until soft. Turn up the heat and add the meat, stirring until it is well browned.

Drain off any fat and add the tomato paste, bouillon cubes and flour. Mix well and cook for a minute before adding the wine and water. Season well with salt and pepper and add the tarragon. Simmer gently for 15 minutes.

Meanwhile cook and mash the potatoes. Add the butter and milk, and season with salt and pepper.

Put the meat mixture in a large well-greased soufflé or baking dish. Spread the corn over the meat and the mashed potatoes on top so that the meat and corn are completely covered. Sprinkle the cheese over the potatoes and bake uncovered for 35 minutes. Place under the broiler for a few minutes to brown the top and serve.

N.B.: The addition of corn is not strictly authentic. However, it looks decorative and adds a nice flavor.

◈ Boiled Beef with Carrots and Dumplings

This is a classic English dish and has always been purported to be a particular favorite of the London cockney. *Serves 6.*

7 bacon slices
3 pounds rolled brisket
1¼ cups ale
1¼ cups Meat Stock
½ cup wine vinegar
10 small white onions
10 carrots, peeled and cut into 4-inch slices
DUMPLINGS:
1 cup flour
½ teaspoon baking powder
½ teaspoon salt
½ cup chopped suet
1 egg
Approximately 4 tablespoons water

Place the bacon slices at the bottom of a large casserole and put the brisket on top. Cover with the ale, stock and vinegar and bring to a boil. Remove any scum. Cover the casserole and place it in the oven. Cook at 250° for 2½ hours. Add the onions and carrots and cook for another hour.

Meanwhile, prepare the dumplings: Sift the flour, baking powder and salt into a large bowl. Add the suet and rub the mixture together with your fingers until it resembles coarse breadcrumbs.

Beat the egg and add it to the mixture. Gradually add enough water to form a dough and shape it into 1-inch balls.

When the meat and vegetables are tender, take them out of the casserole and arrange them on a large serving dish. Cover and keep warm in the oven.

Drop the dumplings into the remaining stock and cook them on top of the stove for 10 to 15 minutes or until they have fluffed out and risen to the surface. Transfer the dumplings to the serving plate and arrange them beside the meat and the vegetables.

Drain the stock into a gravy boat and serve it with the meat and vegetables.

◫ Chiddingly Hot Pot

An all-in-one stew from Chiddingly, a village in Sussex. *Serves 6.*

2 pounds stewing beef, cut into 1-inch cubes
2 tablespoons flour
2 tablespoons oil
1 celery stalk, finely chopped
2 medium-sized onions, finely chopped
Salt
Freshly ground black pepper
2 medium-sized potatoes, sliced in rounds
3 cloves
1 tablespoon tarragon vinegar
1 ounce melted butter
Approximately 2 cups Meat Stock

Preheat the oven to 325°.

Dust the meat with flour and brown it in the oil in a frying pan over low heat. Remove the meat and fry the celery and onions in the same pan for 3 minutes.

Put a layer of onions and celery in the bottom of a deep casserole, then a layer of meat and after that a layer of potatoes. Season each layer with salt and pepper and add the cloves and vinegar. Repeat the layers and finish with a layer of potatoes. Brush them with the melted butter and add enough stock to reach just below the potatoes.

Cover the casserole and cook for 1½ hours. Remove the cover and cook for an additional ½ hour to brown the potatoes.

◪ Guard of Honor with Herb Pudding

A Guard of Honor is a simple but decorative variation of a crown roast and was a favorite dish in Edwardian times. The lamb chops are trimmed and crisscrossed like swords at a military wedding and the herb pudding is placed inside the hollow cavity in the middle. Serve with Brussels sprouts and <u>Mint Sauce</u> or <u>Red Currant Jelly</u>. *Serves 8.*

2 racks of lamb (6 or 7 chops each)
Salt
Freshly ground black pepper
1 teaspoon rosemary
1 tablespoon oil
2 ounces butter
½ cup sherry
HERB PUDDING:
¾ cup oatmeal
½ cup flour
1 teaspoon baking powder
½ cup fresh white breadcrumbs
½ cup shredded suet
½ teaspoon salt
¼ teaspoon pepper
2 teaspoons chopped parsley
*2 teaspoons chopped fresh herbs or ½ teaspoon mixed
   dried herbs*
1 egg
Milk, to mix (approximately ½ cup)
1 onion, finely chopped
¼ cup chopped almonds

Preheat the oven to 350°.

Ask the butcher to skin the rack of lamb and trim the first 1½ inches off the ends of the chops.

Score the outside in diamonds and rub in the salt, pepper and rosemary.

Stand the chops on their ends and push them together so that the exposed bones cross each other alternately. Skewer the meat together at either end across the bottom and coat the outside with the oil and butter. Cover the tops with aluminum foil to prevent their burning. Roast for 30 minutes.

Baste with sherry and continue to cook for another 30 minutes, basting from time to time.

While the meat is cooking, prepare the herb pudding. Mix all the ingredients together, using enough milk to make a fine consistency. Pour a little of the hot oil from the meat into an ovenproof dish and put in the mixture. Cook the pudding for 30 minutes in the oven with the meat.

When the Guard of Honor is cooked, remove the aluminum foil and spoon the herb pudding into the central cavity.

TO CARVE: Cut down between each chop, allowing 2 chops per person.

▨ Reform Cutlets

Reform Cutlets—lamb cutlets (or chops as they are more often called in this country) served with Reform Sauce—were the invention of Francatelli, who was Queen Victoria's head chef until 1852, when he became the chef at the Reform Club, the foremost political club of its day and one that has always had a reputation for excellent food. Reform Cutlets are still a favorite at many clubs today. The sauce has a rich, piquant flavor that is distinctive and unusual. Serve with a green salad. *Serves 6.*

REFORM SAUCE:
2 ounces butter
2 medium-sized carrots, cut into strips
1 medium-sized onion, finely chopped
1 crushed garlic clove
2 ounces cooked ham, cut into small cubes
5 cloves
1 bayleaf
¼ teaspoon mace
½ teaspoon thyme
1 tablespoon chopped parsley
1 cup red wine
1½ cups Meat Stock
4 tablespoons Red Currant Jelly
2 tablespoons arrowroot

12 small lamb rib chops
2 eggs
2 ounces cooked ham, cut into small cubes
2 tablespoons chopped parsley
2 cups fresh white breadcrumbs
Salt
Freshly ground black pepper
2 tablespoons oil

First make the sauce: Melt the butter in a saucepan and add the vegetables, garlic, ham, cloves and herbs. Sauté for a few minutes and add the wine and stock. Bring the mixture to a boil, cover and simmer for 30 minutes. Add the Red Currant Jelly. As soon as it has dissolved, remove the saucepan from the heat.

Strain the liquid through a sieve and press the vegetables down with a wooden spoon to extract all the juice. Discard the vegetables.

Place the arrowroot in the top of a double boiler and add a small amount of the strained stock. Keep stirring while the sauce begins to thicken; heat slowly. Gradually add the rest of the stock and continue to stir until the sauce is well thickened. Keep it warm over very low heat.

Trim the chops of any fat. Beat the eggs and place them in a small bowl. Mix the ham with the parsley and breadcrumbs in another bowl. Season each chop with salt and pepper and dip first in the eggs and then in the breadcrumb mixture, making sure that each chop is well coated.

Heat the oil in a large frying pan and sauté the chops for approximately 12 minutes, turning them from side to side until they are golden brown.

Transfer to a serving dish and serve with the Reform Sauce, which should be placed in a sauceboat or a small pitcher.

▣ Lancashire Hot Pot

Serves 6.

6 shoulder lamb chops
6 lamb kidneys (optional)
1 cup mushrooms, sliced lengthwise
6 medium-sized potatoes, peeled and thinly sliced in rounds
3 medium-sized onions, thinly sliced
Salt
Freshly ground black pepper
1 ounce butter
¼ cup chopped parsley

Preheat the oven to 400°.

Using a casserole at least 6 inches deep, spread the meat, mushrooms, potatoes and onions in layers, seasoning each layer with salt and pepper. Finish with a layer of potatoes and make sure that the slices overlap and look neat. Brush the potatoes with a little butter.

Pour in enough water to come halfway up the pot; cover the pot and place it in the oven for about 30 minutes. Reduce the heat to 275° and cook for another 2 hours, removing the lid for the last ½ hour of cooking time so that the potatoes can brown.

Remove from oven, sprinkle with parsley and serve.

▣ Irish Stew

Irish Stew, known to many families as "White Stew," is very simple to prepare and makes a welcome change from the richer, more sophisticated brown stews. It is traditional to serve it with boiled carrots and red cabbage, but these should be cooked separately. *Serves 4–6.*

3 pounds neck of lamb
6 medium-sized potatoes, peeled and cut in half
4 medium-sized onions, coarsely chopped
1 teaspoon thyme
Salt
Freshly ground black pepper
2 cups water

Preheat the oven to 325°.

Remove excess fat and gristle from the lamb and cut it into small cubes. Put these with the potatoes and onions in layers in a casserole, ending with a layer of potatoes. Sprinkle each layer with a little thyme, salt and pepper. Add the water and cover the pot with a layer of foil pulled tightly across the top and with a well-fitting lid to prevent any evaporation from taking place.

Cook for 2½ hours.

▨ Oxtail Stew

It's hard to understand why oxtails are considered unfashionable since they make wonderful soups and stews and are also economical. This recipe is simple to prepare and very tasty. Serve with baked potatoes and Sherried Puree of Peas. *Serves 8.*

2 ounces lard
2 oxtails, cut into 2-inch pieces
2 tablespoons flour
2 medium-sized onions, coarsely chopped
1 bayleaf
½ teaspoon thyme
3 sprigs parsley
½ teaspoon crushed peppercorns
1 teaspoon allspice
3 small turnips, peeled and coarsely chopped
5 carrots, cut into 3-inch pieces
3 leeks, washed, trimmed and cut into 1-inch slices
Salt

Preheat the oven to 300°.

Melt the lard in a good-sized casserole and allow it to get very hot. Add the oxtails sprinkled with flour and brown them on all sides. Once they have browned, remove them and set them aside.

Fry the onions in the lard until they are golden brown but not burned. Return the oxtails to the pot and add the herbs, parsley, peppercorns and allspice. Add 3 cups of water and bring to a boil. Put in the turnips, carrots and leeks. Cover the pot and cook it in the oven for 1¼ hours.

Remove the stew from the oven and take off the lid. Cool the stew and skim off the fat, check the seasoning, add salt if necessary. Reheat and serve.

◫ Curate's Cheek

This recipe was given to me by an aged curate who lived near Carlisle. Incredibly quick and simple to prepare, it is fit for a bishop or any other important guest who arrives on short notice. The brown sugar and mustard combine to make a wonderfully piquant sauce for the ham. Serve it with wild rice and a salad. *Serves 4.*

1 cup dark brown sugar
3½ tablespoons English mustard powder
1 pound cooked ham, thickly sliced
1 cup heavy cream
1 bunch watercress

Preheat the oven to 300°.

Mix the sugar and mustard in a small bowl. Place the ham in a small ovenproof dish and sprinkle about a tablespoon of the mustard and sugar mixture over each slice. Put any remaining mustard and sugar over the top slice and add the cream.

Bake covered for 20 minutes and then uncovered for another 10.

Put a little watercress on each plate before serving.

◫ Penny's Pork with Chestnuts

Serves 4.

1 pound chestnuts
1 pound boneless pork loin, cut into 1-inch cubes
2 ounces butter
½ teaspoon sage
1 clove garlic, finely chopped
1 cup red wine
¾ cup hot water
Salt
Freshly ground black pepper

Preheat the oven to 300°.

Follow the directions for skinning chestnuts given in the recipe for Chestnut Soup.

Remove any fat or gristle from the pork. Melt the butter in a casserole and gently brown the meat. Add the sage, garlic, wine, water, chestnuts and a generous amount of salt and pepper. Cover and cook in the oven for 2 hours, stirring from time to time.

Serve with rice.

◫ Marbled Veal

This recipe is probably the closest equivalent to a terrine that can be found in the British cuisine. The combination of different meats that are separately layered gives a distinctive marbled effect. I have always found that this dish tastes even better the second time around—so be happy if you have leftovers.

Serve slices of Marbled Veal garnished with a little watercress as a first course. Alternatively, serve it accompanied by a selection of salads for lunch or a light dinner. *Serves 6–8.*

¾ *pound ground veal*
¾ *pound ground loin of pork*
3 tablespoons chopped chives or chopped scallions
Grated rind of one lemon
2 eggs
¼ *pound extra-fat loin of pork*
½ *pound cooked tongue*
1 teaspoon gelatin dissolved in 3 tablespoons hot water
Salt
Freshly ground black pepper
4 tablespoons chopped parsley

Preheat the oven to 350°.

Mix the ground veal and pork in a bowl. Add the chives and lemon rind. Beat the eggs and use them to bind the mixture.

Cut the extra-fat pork and the tongue into ¼-inch cubes and add them and the dissolved gelatin to the ground-meat mixture. Season generously with salt and pepper.

Butter a loaf pan just large enough to hold the mixture. Spoon it into the pan in layers, place a little parsley between layers and end with a layer of meat. Cover the top with aluminum foil and stand the pan in a pot of water. The water should come halfway up the sides of the pan.

Cook for 1½ hours. Remove from the oven and allow to cool.

Cover the pan with a wooden board and place a heavy weight on top. Refrigerate for at least 4 hours.

Remove the board and the foil, run a knife gently around the edges, carefully lift out the loaf and transfer it to a serving dish. Trim off any fat that may have congealed and stuck to the sides. Refrigerate until ready to serve.

Just before serving cut into thin slices.

◪ Veal, Ham and Egg Pie

In years gone by there was a time when butchers would prepare their own meat pies. Alas, there are very few of them left. Today most pies that are for sale are mass-produced, and although some of them are very good, they do not compare with a homemade pie. Although it might seem somewhat daunting and time-consuming, it really isn't difficult to prepare your own.

Hot-water pastry (a pastry made with hot water and not rolled out but simply stretched into shape by hand) is always used for cold meat pies. It is very strong and can absorb the meat juices during the long cooking time without cracking and remain crisp on the outside at the same time. I have found the easiest way to make a meat pie is to cook it in a disposable aluminum-foil loaf pan that can be cut away from the pie after it has been cooked. This eliminates having to lift the pie out and risk having it stick to the bottom. This recipe calls for a standard 1½ quart loaf pan.

Serve for lunch with a tomato salad and Chutney. *Serves 4–6.*

HOT WATER PASTRY:
3 cups flour
Pinch of salt
¼ teaspoon confectioners' sugar
4 ounces lard
½ cup water
2 tablespoons milk
1 egg, beaten

FILLING:
10 ounces stewing veal
10 ounces cooked ham
½ teaspoon salt
½ teaspoon freshly ground black pepper
1 tablespoon chopped parsley
Grated rind and juice of half a lemon
1 teaspoon thyme
¼ teaspoon sage
2 peeled hard-boiled eggs

JELLIED STOCK:
1 cup Chicken Stock
½ envelope unflavored gelatin (½ tablespoon)

TO PREPARE THE PASTRY: Sift the flour, salt and confectioners' sugar into a bowl. Place the lard in a small saucepan with the water and milk and bring to a boil. Remove and pour the liquid over the flour mixture. Using a wooden spoon, stir it as quickly as possible until it forms a dough. Cut off ¼ of the dough and set it aside.

Place the rest of the pastry dough in a loaf pan (see the note in the recipe description), which should be lightly greased. Using your fingers, pull the pastry up around the sides of the pan, being careful to leave no cracks and making sure that it is evenly distributed. Leave any excess pastry hanging over the edges.

Cut the veal and the ham into ¼-inch cubes. Place these in a bowl and mix in all of the other pie ingredients except the eggs.

Spread a layer of the meat on top of the pastry, place the 2 eggs lengthwise one after the other in the pan and cover with the rest of the meat.

Roll out the remaining pastry and place it over the top of the pie, having first dampened the edges with water. Press it down firmly with your fingers, cut away the excess pastry and pinch down the edges with a fork.

Cut a small hole in the middle of the pastry and make a funnel out of a piece of aluminum foil. Place it 1 inch deep in the hole to prevent it from closing while cooking. It is traditional to decorate the top of the pie with a few leaves made out of the leftover pastry bits. When you have done this, brush the top of the pie with beaten egg and put the pan on a baking sheet in a 350° oven. After 30 minutes, turn down the oven to 300° and cook for another hour. Keep an eye on the pastry lid. If it browns too quickly, cover it with a piece of aluminum foil.

Remove the pie from the oven and allow it to cool for 5 minutes. Gently ease it out of the pan or, if you are using a foil pan, take a pair of scissors and gently cut it down the corners before removing.

Heat the Chicken Stock and add the gelatin. When it has completely dissolved and the mixture has cooled a little, pour the stock through the funnel very slowly so that it has time to seep into the pie without overflowing onto the pastry lid.

Remove the funnel and allow the pie to cool before placing it in the refrigerator. Chill for several hours.

Cut the pie into slices about ½-inch thick and place them on a platter surrounded by watercress.

⊠ Melton Mowbray Pork Pie

Melton Mowbray in Warickshire is famous as the pie center of England. The distinctive mark of a Melton Mowbray Pork Pie is the slight hint of anchovy. *Serves 4–6.*

HOT WATER PASTRY:
(See recipe for Veal, Ham and Egg Pie)
FILLING:
1 pound boneless pork shoulder
1 teaspoon chopped sage
½ teaspoon nutmeg
1 teaspoon anchovy paste
1 teaspoon salt
½ teaspoon freshly ground black pepper
8 bacon slices
JELLIED STOCK:
(See recipe for Veal, Ham and Egg Pie)

Dice the pork into ¼-inch cubes. Place them in a bowl and stir in the seasonings. Line the base of the pastry with the bacon slices and fill with the pork. Continue to prepare and cook the pie following the directions given for the Veal, Ham and Egg Pie.

◩ Hindle Wakes

Hindle Wakes is a very old recipe thought to have been brought to Lancashire by the Flemish weavers who arrived there during the fourteenth century. In the north of England it was the custom for each parish church to celebrate its own special festival or saint's day. This would be preceded by a wake in the church, at which time Hindle Wakes or *hen de la wake* would be served.

Although the recipe is time-consuming, it isn't really complicated, and since it is served cold it is an excellent dish to prepare ahead of time for a dinner party. Serve it with rice and a green salad. Don't be put off by the seemingly odd combination of chicken, prunes and a lemon and vinegar sauce. The result is unusually sophisticated. *Serves 6–8.*

1 large (5–6-pound) or 2 small (2–3-pound) chickens, cut up
Giblets from the chicken
2 tablespoons salt
1 large onion, stuck with 3 cloves
1 bayleaf
3 parsley sprigs
4 cups of water
1 cup malt vinegar
1 tablespoon brown sugar
15 large pitted prunes
3 cups cold tea
1¼ cups freshly made toasted breadcrumbs
½ teaspoon each sage, parsley, marjoram and thyme
Juice and grated rind of 2 lemons
2 ounces butter
½ cup flour
Salt
Freshly ground black pepper
1 cup heavy cream
1 lemon cut into circular slices

Put the chicken pieces in a deep saucepan. Add the giblets, salt, onion, bayleaf, parsley, water, vinegar and brown sugar. The chicken pieces should be just covered by the liquid; if they are not, add a little more water.

Bring to a boil and skim. Reduce the heat and simmer for 1 hour. Remove the chicken and allow to cool; reserve the stock.

Meanwhile, soak the prunes in the tea for at least 3 hours. Mix the breadcrumbs with the sage, parsley, marjoram, thyme and the juice and grated rind of 1 lemon. Cut each prune lengthwise down the middle and place a little of the breadcrumb mixture in each. Place the prunes in a large ovenproof pan and bake in a 300° oven for 30 minutes.

In a heavy saucepan, melt the butter over low heat, stir in the flour and cook for at least 5 minutes. Strain the stock in which the chicken pieces were cooked and add 2 to 3 cups of stock to the flour, stirring until you have a thick sauce. Add the juice and rind of the second lemon and salt and pepper to taste. Remove from heat. When the sauce has cooled, stir in the cream. Skin the chicken, remove it from the bones and place on a large serving dish. Spoon the sauce over the chicken until it is completely covered. Place a circle of prunes around the edge of the plate and decorate with the lemon slices. Keep covered until ready to serve, but do not refrigerate as this dish should be served at room temperature.

▨ Stoved Chicken

This traditional Scottish country recipe, also known as Chicken Stovies, is similar to Irish Stew in that the trick in cooking it successfully is to prevent as much evaporation as possible from taking place. *Serves 4–6.*

2 ounces butter
6 chicken pieces (approximately 3 pounds)
5 medium-sized potatoes, peeled and sliced in 1/4-inch thick
    rounds
2 large onions, sliced in rounds
Salt
Freshly ground black pepper
1 cup Chicken Stock
3 tablespoons chopped parsley

Preheat the oven to 275°.

Melt half the butter in a casserole and lightly brown the chicken on both sides over medium heat. Set aside the chicken and place a layer of potatoes on the bottom of the dish. Follow with alternate layers of onion, chicken and potatoes, ending with a layer of potatoes. Salt and pepper each layer and dot with knobs of the remaining butter.

Pour the stock on top and cover the casserole first with foil and then with a lid. Bring the mixture to the boiling point, then place the dish in the oven and cook for 2½ hours.

After 2 hours of cooking, check to see that the chicken is still moist. If it appears to be drying up, add a little more Chicken Stock. Remove the foil and the lid for the last ½ hour of cooking and brush the potatoes with butter so they will brown.

Sprinkle with parsley before serving.

◨ Coronation Chicken

This recipe for what is really a cold, curried chicken was invented in honor of Queen Elizabeth II's coronation in 1953. The coronation ceremony at Westminster Abbey was extremely long, and at one point during the proceedings, the queen and her ladies-in-waiting are reputed to have slipped behind the scenes and fortified themselves with a quick helping of Coronation Chicken. Serve chilled with cold rice and a salad. *Serves 4–6.*

1 cooked chicken (about 3 pounds)
1 medium-sized onion, finely chopped
1 tablespoon olive oil
1 tablespoon curry powder
½ cup Chicken Stock
2 teaspoons tomato puree
Juice of half a lemon
2 tablespoons Tomato or Mango Chutney
½ cup mayonnaise
½ cup heavy cream

Flake the chicken into small, bite-sized pieces and set aside. Soften the onion in the oil in a saucepan over low heat until it is soft but not brown. Add the curry powder and cook for a few minutes. Then add the stock, tomato puree, lemon juice and chutney.

Stir until the mixture comes to a boil, simmer for 5 minutes and puree in a blender or food processor. Allow the mixture to cool and add the mayonnaise and cream.

Place the chicken pieces on a serving dish and spoon the sauce over the chicken.

◩ Roast Chicken with Cranberry Stuffing

The cranberry originally came from England and was taken to America by the first settlers. It used to grow in the fens around Cambridge. However, once these swamps were drained, the cranberry no longer flourished there and has become exceedingly rare. It is now found only in a few remote parts of Northern England and Scotland. As there is no such scarcity of cranberries in this country, I find myself frequently using this recipe. The stuffing has a wonderfully tart flavor, and its deep pink color makes this a very decorative dish. Serve with peas and new potatoes. *Serves 4–6.*

1 roasting chicken (about 4 pounds)
2 ounces butter
2 teaspoons rosemary
CRANBERRY STUFFING:
4 tablespoons sugar
4 tablespoons water
2 cups fresh cranberries
1½ cups fresh white breadcrumbs
1 small onion, finely chopped
2 tablespoons chopped parsley
Grated rind of 1 lemon
Salt
Freshly ground black pepper

Preheat oven to 375°.

Wipe the chicken, rub salt into its cavities and set it aside.

Put the sugar and the water in a saucepan. Stir over low heat until the sugar has dissolved. Add the cranberries and bring to a boil. Cook briskly until the skins pop and then simmer for 5 minutes.

Mix the breadcrumbs, onion, parsley and lemon rind in a bowl. Add the cranberries and salt and pepper to taste.

Spoon the stuffing into the chicken, both in the main cavity and in the neck end. Pull the neck skin over and secure with a skewer. Close the main cavity with a skewer and tie the legs together with a piece of string.

Place the chicken in a roasting pan and rub it all over with the butter and rosemary. Cover the breast with aluminum foil, place the chicken in the oven and roast, allowing 20 minutes per pound. Baste occasionally and remove the foil for the last half hour of cooking.

◧ Fried Chicken with Gubbins Sauce

Nathaniel Gubbins, an author and gourmet who lived at the turn of the century, is credited with inventing this mustard sauce for fried chicken. It is excellent, but beware, it is hot. Serve this dish with rice and a generous side helping of <u>Chutney</u>. *Serves 4–6.*

3 tablespoons oil
6 chicken pieces
Salt
Freshly ground black pepper
1 teaspoon rosemary
2 tablespoons parsley, finely chopped
GUBBINS SAUCE:
2 ounces butter
3 tablespoons freshly prepared English mustard
2 tablespoons tarragon vinegar
2 cups sour cream

Melt the oil in a large frying pan. Sprinkle the chicken pieces with salt and pepper and place them in the pan. Add the rosemary and cook over medium heat for 25 minutes, turning the chicken frequently.

While the chicken is cooking, melt the butter in a double boiler and add the mustard. Stir in the vinegar very slowly and add the sour cream gradually.

When the chicken is cooked, transfer it to a warm serving dish, pour the sauce over it and sprinkle the parsley on top.

▣ Miss McFarlane's Honey-Glazed Chicken

Serves 4–6.

1 roasting chicken (approximately 4 pounds)
Salt
Freshly ground black pepper
1 large green apple, peeled, cored and quartered
1 large onion, cut in half
4–5 tablespoons oil
4 tablespoons clear honey
1 bunch watercress

Preheat the oven to 325°.

Sprinkle the inside of the chicken with salt and pepper. Place the apple and onion in the cavity. Shut the opening with a skewer and tie the legs together with a piece of string.

Brush the chicken with oil and place it in a roasting pan. Season with salt and pepper and spread 2 tablespoons of honey on top.

Roast, allowing 20 minutes per pound. Baste frequently and spread the last 2 tablespoons of honey over the chicken after it has cooked for 45 minutes.

Arrange on a serving dish and garnish with watercress.

◻ Roast Goose with Sage and Onion Stuffing

There is an old British custom that goose should be eaten on Michaelmas Day. One version of how this originated is that Elizabeth I was eating goose when she received the news of the defeat of the Spanish Armada. She promptly issued a royal decree, declaring that roast goose should henceforth be served on Michaelmas Day (September 29) to commemorate this great British victory.

The tradition of Michaelmas goose is dying out and has been replaced by the Christmas goose, which is now more popular than turkey. Serve Roast Goose with Plum Sauce and Brussels Sprouts with Chestnuts. *Serves 6–8.*

ONION STUFFING:
2 ounces butter
3 large onions, finely chopped
½ pound minced veal or pork
10 fresh sage leaves, finely chopped, or 1 teaspoon dried sage
2 cups fresh white breadcrumbs
1 egg
¼ cup slivered almonds
1 cup milk
Salt
Freshly ground black pepper

1 goose (approximately 8–10 pounds)
1 ounce butter
1½ tablespoons flour
Salt
Freshly ground black pepper
½ cup white wine
2 cups Chicken Stock or stock made from the goose giblets

Preheat the oven to 350°.

TO PREPARE THE STUFFING: Melt the butter in a small frying pan and sauté the onions until they are soft. Mix all the other stuffing ingredients together in a bowl, add the onions and season generously with salt and pepper.

Remove any fat from inside the goose, stuff it and truss it. Place it on a rack in a roasting pan and lightly prick the skin in several places with a fork. Rub it with the butter and half a tablespoon of the flour, then sprinkle with salt and pepper. Pour the wine into the pan and roast the goose for 1 hour, basting it every 15 minutes.

After 1 hour, pour out ¾ of the fat that has accumulated in the pan. (Keep it for later use; it is the purest of all frying fats.) Reprick the skin and return the goose to the oven for another hour, or if it weighs over 9 pounds, another 1½ hours.

Transfer the cooked bird to a serving dish. Remove all the fat in the pan but leave the juices. Mix in the remaining flour to make a roux over low heat and add the stock to make gravy.

◪ Roast Pheasant

If you are lucky enough to come by a brace of pheasants, there is nothing so enjoyable or festive as roast pheasant. Serve it with a generous amount of Bread Sauce. *Serves 4–6.*

3 ounces butter
3 tablespoons flour
1 brace of pheasant
1 teaspoon sage
4 bacon slices
1 bunch watercress
1 small onion, finely chopped
½ cup mushrooms, finely sliced
1 cup sherry
1 cup Meat Stock
Salt
Freshly ground black pepper

Preheat the oven to 400°.

Melt 2 ounces of butter in a roasting pan. Sprinkle 2 tablespoons of flour over the pheasants and gently brown them over medium heat for 2 or 3 minutes. Put half of the remaining butter and the sage inside each pheasant.

Put the pheasants breast up in the roasting pan and cover with the bacon slices. Roast the birds for 35 minutes, basting from time to time. Be careful not to overcook them or they will become dry.

Transfer the cooked pheasants to a warm serving dish, surround them with watercress and let them rest for at least 10 minutes before carving.

Spoon out most of the cooking fat from the roasting pan, leaving just enough to brown the onion in. Place the pan over the fire and when the onion has turned soft and brown, add the mushrooms and toss for a few minutes. Add the remaining tablespoon of flour and gradually pour in the sherry and the stock.

Bring the mixture to a boil and simmer for 10 minutes. Remove any scum, season to taste with salt and pepper and serve in a gravy boat.

⊠ Dorothy Ballam's Poacher's Pie

This recipe was recently sent to me by a friend of a friend. I had thought about including a rabbit pie in this book but had decided against it since rabbits are not an everyday item on most meat counters in this country. However, when Mrs. Ballam's recipe arrived, it looked so good that I changed my mind. Incidentally, chicken can be substituted for rabbit; but if you do this I don't think you could still legitimately refer to this dish as Poacher's Pie. *Serves 4.*

1 bayleaf
8 bacon slices
1 pound mushrooms, sliced lengthwise
3 leeks, cleaned and chopped into 1-inch rounds
1 rabbit (about 2 pounds), cut into small portions
Salt
Freshly ground black pepper
3 tablespoons chopped parsley
3 medium-sized potatoes, peeled and sliced into ¼-inch rounds
1 tablespoon vinegar

Preheat the oven to 325°.

Place the bayleaf on the bottom of a large, heavy ovenproof dish. Place 4 slices of bacon over the bayleaf and cover with half the mushrooms and half the leeks. Put the rabbit pieces on top and cover with the remaining mushrooms and leeks. Season heavily with salt and pepper and sprinkle on 2 tablespoons of the chopped parsley. Place the potatoes over the top so that the other vegetables are completely covered. Add a little more salt and pepper and the rest of the parsley. Put the remaining bacon slices on top and pour the vinegar over them.

Put a tight lid on the pot and cook for 2 hours. Resist the urge to look at the pie while it is cooking as uncovering it will result in a loss of the natural juices.

⊠ Mixed Grill

Mixed Grill is without a doubt one of the most successful culinary inventions of this century. For those who no longer have the time to eat a large breakfast every morning but miss it all the same, a mixed grill, which brings the best of breakfast to the dinner table, is a perfect solution. *Serves 6.*

4 ounces melted butter
6 sausages
6 kidneys
2 cups button mushrooms
6 small steaks
6 tomatoes, halved
6 bacon slices
1 bunch watercress

Heat the broiler and brush all the ingredients except the watercress with the melted butter. Broil the sausages, kidneys and mushrooms and then keep them warm while you broil the steaks, tomatoes and bacon.

Arrange the mixed grill on a serving dish, garnish with the watercress and serve.

▧ Skuets

This is an old English method of cooking sweetbreads. They are served on skewers in a kebab style—hence the name. Serve with Bread Sauce. *Serves 4.*

1 pound sweetbreads
Salt
1 tablespoon lemon juice
8 slices bacon
12 button mushrooms
2 ounces melted butter
2 tablespoons parsley

TO PREPARE THE SWEETBREADS FOR COOKING: Soak them for 2 hours in a bowl of cold water, to which should be added 1 tablespoon of salt and the lemon juice. Then place them in a saucepan with fresh cold water and bring quickly to a boil. Simmer until the sweetbreads turn an opaque color, remove them from the saucepan and drain under cold water. As soon as they are cool, pull off any gristly bits and as much of the skin as possible.

Cut the sweetbreads into cubes about 1 inch thick and divide them into 4 parts. Cut the bacon into 1-inch pieces and thread the sweetbreads, bacon and mushrooms onto 4 long skewers. Brush them with melted butter, sprinkle with parsley and broil under medium heat for 15 minutes.

Vegetables

Sweet English Peas
Sherried Puree of Peas
Pease Pudding
Glazed Onions
Leeks with Brown Butter
Glazed Carrots
Brussels Sprouts with Chestnuts
Pureed Brussels Sprouts
Braised Parsnips
Roast Potatoes
Stoved Tatties
Teisen Nionod
Pan Haggerty
Punchnep
Bubble and Squeak
Colcannon
Spiced Cabbage
Cabbage with Milk
Cheese Cauliflower
Vicarage Beets

What do the British do to their vegetables? They overdo them! It's all rather perplexing since nowhere else in the world will you find a greater variety of fresh produce in the shops or a greater passion for home-grown vegetables. The array of vegetables exhibited at any country fair or flower show is remarkable, but something terrible happens between the picking and the eating. All too often, the saddest, wettest, weariest-looking vegetables emerge from British kitchens and, not surprisingly, they have become the subject of ridicule the world over.

This was not always the case. Visiting England at the beginning of the nineteenth century, Heinrich Heine was delighted with "the naive English vegetables which come to the table just the way God made them." And cookery books published about that time abound in vegetable recipes and contain adamant warnings about the perils of overboiling and overcooking.

When did the trouble begin? My suspicion is that Nanny probably had something to do with it. She believed that vegetables should be *well* cooked, and under her watchful eye they fast became an object of duty and an exercise in character formation. "Children must eat their vegetables before having their pudding," "Cabbage is good for you," "Carrots make your hair curl and help you to see in the dark." Small wonder that children had to be forced to eat their vegetables.

Now that Nanny is all but gone and a whole generation has grown up free of her admonitions, a new appreciation of vegetables is beginning to emerge. There has been a distinct improvement over the past few years in the way vegetables are cooked and many now arrive at the British table in quite good condition. Once more, the delights of new potatoes, tiny peas, young carrots, glazed onions, braised parsnips and, yes, even cabbage are beginning to reappear.

◫ Sweet English Peas

The combination of sugar and mint in this recipe gives the peas a taste that is quite out of this world. If you cannot get new, small peas, it's not worth buying those dreadful large bullets that appear every summer in most supermarkets. Better by far to substitute small, frozen peas. *Serves 4.*

1 pound peas
2 ounces butter
1 tablespoon chopped fresh mint
1 teaspoon sugar
Salt
Freshly ground black pepper

Cook the peas in a small amount of boiling salted water until they are tender (approximately 2–5 minutes depending on their size). If you are using frozen peas, follow the instructions given on the package. Drain and set aside.

Heat the butter in another saucepan and add the peas, mint and sugar. Toss and cook gently for 2 minutes. Season to taste with salt and pepper and serve.

◪ Sherried Puree of Peas

This recipe is the best way I know to change people's views on peas. Since the peas are only coarsely pureed, they have a very unusual texture, and with nothing but a little sherry added to them they remain a vibrant green color. *Serves 4–6.*

2 pounds fresh or 1½ pounds frozen peas
1 cup sherry
Salt
Freshly ground black pepper

Cook the peas in a small amount of boiling salted water until they are tender (approximately 2–5 minutes depending on their size and age). If you are using frozen peas, follow the instructions given on the package.

Drain the peas and put them in a blender or food processor with the sherry. Puree them very lightly so that some of the peas remain whole.

Return them to the saucepan in which they were cooked. Season to taste with salt and pepper. Reheat very gently so that they do not burn.

◪ Pease Pudding

Pease Pudding hot,
Pease Pudding cold,
Pease Pudding in the pot,
Nine days old.
(Nursery Rhyme)

Pease Pudding comes from Newcastle and is traditionally served with pork or sausages. Try it also with Beef Guinness. *Serves 4–6.*

1 pound split peas
2 ounces butter
2 eggs
Salt
Freshly ground black pepper

Follow the directions given on the package for soaking and cooking split peas.

Once cooked, drain the peas and puree them in a blender or food processor. Mix in the butter and eggs and salt and pepper to taste.

Spoon the mixture into a well-greased 3-cup pudding bowl. Cover tightly with aluminum foil and secure the ends with a piece of string tied around the rim of the bowl. Place the bowl on a steamer rack or on an inverted saucer in a large saucepan containing about 2 inches of water. Cover the saucepan and steam for 1 hour.

Remove the pudding from the pan and take off the string and foil. Serve the Pease Pudding directly from the bowl in which it has been cooked.

(Leftovers can be cut into slices and fried in butter. It sounds ghastly but don't be put off—it's surprisingly good.)

▣ Glazed Onions

It's too bad that onions are so seldom served on their own. Here is a recipe that does justice to this much-neglected vegetable, which is available all the year round and certainly deserves to make at least an occasional solo appearance. *Serves 4–6.*

2 ounces butter
1½ pounds peeled small white onions (approximately 20)
6 tablespoons sugar
*½ cup **Chicken Stock***

Melt the butter in a large heavy-bottomed saucepan until it sizzles. Add the onions and toss them for a few minutes so that they turn slightly brown.

Sprinkle the sugar over the onions and continue to toss them over low heat until they are completely covered with a sticky layer of sugar. Add the stock and simmer uncovered until the stock evaporates, leaving a thick glaze that covers the onions. This will take about 15 minutes. Shake the saucepan from time to time while cooking.

Serve very hot.

◩ Leeks with Brown Butter

Leeks are an ancient vegetable and have been grown in Britain for thousands of years. They are particularly abundant in Wales and are used in many traditional Welsh recipes such as the one given here, which is simple, quick and delicious. *Serves 4.*

6 leeks
3 ounces butter
4 teaspoons toasted breadcrumbs
1 teaspoon lemon juice
Salt

Clean the leeks by washing them in water and cutting away the tops of the green leaves and the roots. Plunge them into a pan of boiling water and boil for 10 minutes. Before removing, test to make sure they are cooked by piercing them with a knife. Drain and place in a serving dish.

Melt the butter in a separate pan and cook until it sizzles and turns a golden brown. Add the breadcrumbs, lemon juice and salt and pour over the leeks.

Serve immediately.

◫ Glazed Carrots

Carrots taste wonderful if correctly cooked. Always buy the smallest, thinnest carrots you can find and be sure not to over-cook them as there is nothing more unappetizing than mushy carrots. This recipe is simple and gives the carrots an unusual caramelized flavor. *Serves 4.*

1 pound carrots, pared and cut into thin 2-inch-long slices
½ cup water
2 ounces butter
3 tablespoons sugar
Salt
Freshly ground black pepper
3 cloves
1 tablespoon parsley

Place the carrots in a wide-bottomed saucepan. Add the water, butter, sugar, a little salt and pepper and the cloves.

Bring to a boil and cook covered at a steady boil for 5 minutes. Continue to cook uncovered until the carrots are tender and the liquid has turned thick and syrupy.

Add the parsley and serve.

◨ Brussels Sprouts with Chestnuts

Brussels Sprouts are traditionally served with roast turkey or goose on Christmas Day. The chestnuts add a distinctive crunchiness and sweetness to the sprouts, and the combination is very festive. *Serves 6–8.*

1 pound chestnuts
1½ pounds Brussels sprouts (the smallest you can find)
Salt
Freshly ground black pepper
2 ounces butter

Follow the directions for skinning chestnuts given in the recipe for <u>Chestnut Soup</u>. Simmer them in a pan of fresh, salted water for 10 to 15 minutes until they are tender. Be careful not to overcook or they will fall apart. Remove the chestnuts from the water, drain, set aside and keep warm.

Remove any damaged outer leaves from the sprouts, trim the stalks and cut a small cross at the bottom of each stalk. Wash and soak them in cold water for 10 minutes. Cook them in a small amount of boiling salted water for 6 to 8 minutes and drain.

Return the sprouts to the pan, add the chestnuts, season to taste with salt and pepper and stir in the butter.

Transfer to a serving dish and keep warm until ready to serve. (If you are preparing this dish ahead of time, wait until you are almost ready to serve before adding the butter.)

◩ Pureed Brussels Sprouts

Serves 4.

1 pound fresh or 2 10-ounce packages frozen Brussels sprouts
1 cup heavy cream
2 ounces butter
Salt
Freshly ground black pepper
¼ teaspoon nutmeg

Follow the directions for preparing and cooking sprouts in
Brussels Sprouts with Chestnuts. Drain and puree them in a
blender or food processor with ½ cup of the cream.

Return the pureed sprouts to the saucepan and stir in the rest
of the cream and the butter. Season to taste with salt and pepper and add the nutmeg.

◪ Braised Parsnips

I often tell 'em how wrong folks are to say that soft
words butter no parsnips and hard words break no bones.
—Barsetshire Chronicles (Trollope)

In the seventeenth century John Evelyn wrote that the "Parsnep . . . is by some thought more nourishing than the Turnep." Today, both these ancient vegetables are somewhat scorned and their very names have a pinched sound, but anyone who has tasted Braised Parsnips will scorn them no more. They are particularly delicious as a complement to Roast Beef and Horseradish Sauce. *Serves 4–6.*

1 pound large parsnips, scraped
3 tablespoons oil
½ cup Chicken Stock
½ teaspoon prepared English mustard

Sliver the parsnips into paper-thin slices with a potato peeler, stopping when you reach the core.

Heat the oil in a frying pan and mix in the stock and the mustard. Add the parsnips and sauté for 2 to 3 minutes, turning frequently.

Serve immediately.

▣ Roast Potatoes

Potatoes were introduced into England from the West Indies in the sixteenth century and in 1664, J. Forster wrote a book entitled *England's Happiness Increased, or a Sure and Easie Remedy against all succeeding Dear Years, by a Plantation of the Roots called Potatoes.*

Roast potatoes should be crisp on the outside and soft on the inside. Unfortunately, all too often they emerge not crisp but soggy. The secret is time and lots of it. It is important to allow at least 1½ hours cooking time. If you are planning to serve roast potatoes with roast meat, start cooking the potatoes ahead of time and add the meat to the same pan when appropriate. *Serves 6.*

8 medium-sized potatoes, peeled and cut in half lengthwise
Salt
1 tablespoon flour
4 tablespoons meat fat or oil

Preheat the oven to 300°.

Make sure the potatoes are dry. Scratch their surfaces with a fork, then sprinkle them generously with salt and a little flour. Heat the fat or oil in a roasting pan and when it is hot add the potatoes. Cook for 1½ hours, basting and turning from time to time.

⊠ Stoved Tatties

In Scotland potatoes are known as "tatties." Stoved tatties are so called because they are cooked on the stove. *Serves 4–6.*

5 medium-sized potatoes, peeled and sliced thin
3 tablespoons water
Salt
Freshly ground black pepper

Place the potatoes and half the water in a heavy saucepan. Sprinkle with salt and pepper and add the rest of the water. Cover and cook over low heat for 30 minutes, or until the potatoes are soft.

⊠ Teisen Nionod (Welsh Onion Cake)

This is a very old Welsh recipe for a potato and onion dish that is baked like a cake in a slow cooking oven. It is similar to the French recipe for *pommes dauphinoise. Serves 6.*

7 medium-sized potatoes, peeled and sliced in thin rounds
3 medium-sized onions, finely chopped
4 ounces butter
Salt
Freshly ground black pepper

Preheat the oven to 300°.

Dry the potato slices in a towel to remove excess moisture. Grease a loaf or cake pan and place the potatoes and the onions in layers, beginning and ending with a layer of potatoes. Dot each layer with a little butter (but leave at least 1 ounce of the butter to dot over the top layer) and season each layer with a little salt and pepper. Cover with aluminum foil and cook for 1½ hours. Remove the foil cover for the last half hour so that the cake has a chance to brown.

Turn the cake onto an ovenproof serving dish and place under the broiler for a couple of minutes before serving.

⊠ Pan Haggerty

Pan Haggerty is a potato recipe from Northumberland. The name is possibly a corruption of the Anglo Saxon word *haecan,* which means to chop into pieces. Serve with baked ham or cold chicken. *Serves 4–6.*

3 tablespoons bacon fat or oil
4 medium-sized potatoes, peeled and sliced thin
2 medium-sized onions, finely chopped
1 cup grated Cheddar cheese
Salt
Freshly ground black pepper

Melt the fat over low heat in a heavy frying pan and make sure that it covers the entire surface of the pan. Fill the pan with alternate layers of potatoes, onions and cheese, beginning and ending with a layer of potatoes. Season each layer with a little salt and pepper.

Fry gently for about 30 minutes, then broil for 5 to 10 minutes until the top is well browned.

Serve straight from the frying pan.

▣ Punchnep

Another Welsh dish, which combines potatoes and turnips to make a delicious buttery puree. It goes well with cold ham or tongue. *Serves 6.*

1 pound potatoes, peeled
1 pound small turnips, peeled
3 ounces butter
Salt
Freshly ground black pepper
5 tablespoons cream

Boil the potatoes and the turnips in separate saucepans until they are tender. Drain and mash them separately and divide the butter between them. (It is important not to mix them until each has been mashed separately.) At this point, combine them. Season to taste with salt and pepper, beat thoroughly and put in a warm dish. Make several holes in the puree with the end of a wooden spoon. Pour the cream into the holes and serve very hot.

◪ Bubble and Squeak

This recipe gets its name from the bubbling and squeaking that takes place while it is cooking. Bubble and Squeak was much in evidence during the Depression, since it is an economical dish and also an excellent way of using leftover vegetables. Bits of cold meat can be added to the basic recipe. Serve with Wow-Wow Sauce. *Serves 6.*

4 cups cooked mashed potatoes
4 cups cooked cabbage, chopped into small pieces
Salt
Freshly ground black pepper
4 tablespoons olive oil

Mix the potatoes and cabbage and season well with salt and pepper.

Heat the oil in a large frying pan and add the vegetables. Sauté over medium heat, pressing down the vegetables so that they form the shape of a flat cake. When one side is well browned, turn and cook on the other side.

Transfer to a hot serving plate and serve immediately.

◙ Colcannon

Colcannon is a Scottish variation of Bubble and Squeak, which has scallions in it and is cooked in the oven instead of in a frying pan. It was the custom at Halloween for the cook to place some charms and thimbles in the Colcannon; those who were lucky enough to find a charm in their helping could be sure of good luck. *Serves 6.*

6 scallions
⅔ cup milk
4 cups cooked mashed potatoes
4 cups cooked cabbage, chopped into small pieces
Salt
Freshly ground black pepper
4 ounces butter

Preheat the oven to 350°.

Chop the scallions very fine, using both the white and the green parts, and put them in a small saucepan with the milk. Bring to just below the boiling point and set aside.

Mix the potatoes and cabbage in a mixing bowl. Season with salt and pepper, pour in the milk and scallions and mix well together. Transfer to a greased pudding bowl or soufflé dish and bake for 20 minutes in the oven.

Turn onto a serving dish. Make several holes in the top and put a knob of butter in each hole. Serve immediately.

▣ Spiced Cabbage

A visitor to England once remarked that the English have only three vegetables and two of them are cabbage. Although cabbage has probably been more brutalized by overcooking than any other vegetable, if correctly cooked it can be delicious. This recipe brings out its naturally sweet flavor. *Serves 6.*

1 large cabbage (approximately 2 pounds)
2 medium-sized onions, finely chopped
2 medium-sized apples, peeled, cored and cut into ½-inch cubes
1 ounce butter
½ teaspoon cinnamon
Salt
Freshly ground black pepper

Shred or chop the cabbage very fine and plunge it into a saucepan that contains 4 cups of boiling, salted water. Boil covered for 3 minutes, drain and set aside.

Fry the onions and apples in the butter until they are soft. Sprinkle with cinnamon, add the cabbage and toss over low heat for 2 minutes. Season to taste with salt and pepper, transfer to a serving dish and serve.

◪ Cabbage with Milk

This is another recipe that convincingly makes the case for how good cabbage can be. Serve it with Veal, Ham and Egg Pie. *Serves 6.*

1 large cabbage (approximately 2 pounds)
½ cup milk
2 ounces butter
Salt
Freshly ground black pepper

Chop the cabbage coarsely. Bring a large pan of salted water to a boil and plunge the cabbage into it for 2 minutes. Drain and return to the pan. Add the milk and half the butter, season lightly with salt and pepper, cover and simmer for approximately 15 minutes.

Transfer the cabbage to a serving dish, stir in the remaining butter and serve.

◙ Cheese Cauliflower

Cheese Cauliflower has never stopped paying the price for its overfrequent appearance on institutional menus, where it has a reputation for arriving at the table overcooked, tasteless and blanketed in a ghastly, undercooked, lumpy sauce. However, there is a world of difference between such a horror and a well-prepared, creamy, golden, delicately flavored Cheese Cauliflower, which makes an excellent lunch or supper dish. Try serving it with cold meat—it does wonders for leftover turkey. *Serves 4.*

1 good-sized cauliflower
3 cups Basic White Sauce
¼ teaspoon nutmeg
1½ cups grated Cheddar cheese
1 cup freshly made breadcrumbs
1 ounce butter
Salt
Freshly ground black pepper

Remove the outside stalks from the cauliflower. Slit the stem in several places and steam in a small amount of salted water for about 15 minutes or until the flowerets are tender but not mushy. (You should be able to pierce the stem with a knife.) Drain and set aside but do not allow to cool.

In the meantime, prepare the white sauce and when it is ready add the nutmeg and cheese. Simmer over very low heat until the cheese has fully melted.

Sauté the breadcrumbs in the butter until they are crisp and golden.

Cut the cauliflower into small pieces and put it in an oven-proof dish. Season with salt and pepper, pour the cheese sauce over it so that the cauliflower is completely covered and sprinkle the breadcrumbs on top.

Place the dish under the broiler for a few minutes until the sauce is well browned and bubbling. Serve immediately.

◙ Vicarage Beets

Beets, called beetroot in England, are another of those unjustly despised vegetables. Cooked in their skins and served whole and hot they can be awfully good. However, as with most vegetables, the smaller the beet, the better it will taste. Avoid tough, large beets at all costs. *Serves 4.*

1 pound small whole beets
1 tablespoon chopped parsley
1 tablespoon chopped chives
2 ounces butter
Salt

Wash the beets and cut off the stalks but do not remove the skins or they will bleed while cooking. Drop into a saucepan of boiling salted water and cook until they are tender. The amount of time will vary depending on their size and age, but it should take between 40 minutes and 1 hour. To determine whether they are sufficiently cooked, press them gently with your fingers. If the skin comes off easily they are done.

Remove the beets from the saucepan and peel off the skins. Discard cooking water. Return them to the saucepan and toss for a few minutes with the parsley, chives and butter.

Season to taste with a little salt and serve.

Sauces

Mint Sauce
Horseradish Sauce
Cumberland Sauce
Madeira Sauce
Bread Sauce
Plum Sauce
Wow-Wow Sauce
Hannover Sauce
Basic White Sauce
Parsley Sauce
Anchovy Sauce
Stilton Sauce
Gooseberry Sauce
Mustard Sauce
Egg Sauce
Onion Sauce
Basic Brown Sauce
Caper Sauce
Scrumpy Sauce
Brandy Butter (Hard Sauce)
Cumberland Rum Butter
Custard
Jam Sauce
Melba Sauce

SAUCES INCLUDED IN
THE MEAT SECTION:

Reform Sauce
Gubbins Sauce

"Woe to the cook whose sauce has no sting."
—Chaucer

Sauces are yet another of those well-kept British culinary secrets, and most people are genuinely astonished to learn that there are any British sauces apart from that heavy, lumpy blanket known as White Sauce—the legendary standby of every self-respecting landlady.

In fact, there is a great variety of indigenous British sauces, ranging from sharp, piquant ones such as Cumberland, Gooseberry, Cider, Anchovy and Mustard to the gentler Bread Sauce and marvelously scented fresh herb sauces such as Mint and Horseradish. Sweet sauces include Cumberland Rum Butter, Hard Sauce and the not to be forgotten Custard, which can be delicious but like White Sauce has often suffered at the hands of those same landladies.

◪ Mint Sauce

The most English of all sauces and the simplest to prepare, mint sauce should be served with roast lamb. It also has a quite extraordinary effect on new potatoes. *Makes ¾ cup.*

1 cup fresh mint, chopped very fine
3 tablespoons boiling water
2 tablespoons sugar
4 tablespoons white wine or white wine vinegar

Place the mint in a pitcher or gravy boat and pour the boiling water over it. Wait for 20 minutes so that the mint has time to infuse the water. Add the sugar and wine or wine vinegar. Stir well and serve.

◪ Horseradish Sauce

Serve with hot or cold roast beef. *Makes ¾ cup.*

3 tablespoons fresh grated horseradish or ¼ cup bottled white
  horseradish, drained and squeezed dry
1 teaspoon lemon juice
1 teaspoon wine vinegar
½ teaspoon sugar
¼ teaspoon prepared English mustard
Salt
½ cup heavy cream

Mix the horseradish, lemon juice, vinegar, sugar and mustard in a small bowl and add a pinch of salt. Whip the cream until it is stiff and fold it into the other ingredients.

Chill until needed. It is a good idea to chill horseradish sauce for at least 3 hours before serving.

⊠ Cumberland Sauce

A marvelous strong, rich sauce that is served cold, Cumberland Sauce is dark red in color and tastes superb served with ham, vension or a Veal, Ham and Egg Pie. *Makes 1½ cups.*

Rind and juice of 2 oranges
Rind and juice of 1 lemon
8 ounces Red Currant Jelly
½ cup port
¼ teaspoon mace
½ teaspoon ground ginger

Cut the rind off the oranges and the lemon with a potato peeler, being careful not to include any of the pith. Cut the rind into matchstick strips and place them in a pan. Cover with boiling water and boil for 2 minutes. Strain and set the rind aside.

Squeeze the juice from the oranges and the lemon.

Melt the Red Currant Jelly in a small saucepan over low heat. Add the port, the orange and lemon juice and the spices. Simmer uncovered, stirring from time to time, for 15 minutes. Add the rind and remove from the stove.

Cool and refrigerate until the sauce has thickened.

◨ Madeira Sauce

This sauce does an amazing job of rejuvenating a leftover roast or turkey. It has the added advantage of keeping well; it can be safely refrigerated for 3 to 4 days. *Makes 3 cups.*

1 ounce butter
3 tablespoons onions, finely chopped
1 tablespoon celery, finely chopped
½ cup flour
3½ cups Meat Stock
2 tablespoons diced ham
2 tablespoons chopped parsley
1 teaspoon thyme
¼ cup tomato paste
Salt
Freshly ground black pepper
½ cup Madeira
1 ounce softened butter

Melt the butter in a heavy-bottomed saucepan over low heat and add the onion and celery. Cook until they are soft, add the flour and cook for another 5 minutes, stirring constantly. Gradually add the stock, continuing to stir until you have a smooth sauce. Finally add the ham, parsley, thyme and tomato paste.

Cover the saucepan and simmer gently for 2 hours. Remove from the heat, strain and season to taste with salt and pepper.

Reduce the Madeira to approximately 3 tablespoons by boiling it very fast. Add it to the sauce and stir in the softened butter bit by bit. Reheat and serve.

▨ Bread Sauce

Bread sauce is the traditional British accompaniment to roast chicken, roast turkey or any roast game bird. If you have never eaten bread sauce, don't be put off by its prosaic name. It has an extremely delicate and subtle flavor. Having once tried it, you may even agree with Lady Baden-Powell, the founder of the Girl Guides, who always maintained that the *whole* point of roast chicken was the bread sauce. *Makes 2 cups.*

1 small onion, peeled and studded with 3 cloves
2 cups milk
2½ cups fresh white breadcrumbs
2 tablespoons butter
Pinch of nutmeg
2 tablespoons sour cream
Salt
Freshly ground black pepper

Put the onion and milk in the top of a double boiler and bring very slowly to just below the boiling point. Remove the saucepan from the heat and allow it to stand for 20 minutes, so as to infuse the milk with the flavor of the onion and cloves.

Discard the onion and add the breadcrumbs to the milk. Return to the heat, still using a double boiler. Stir until the sauce thickens. Then stir in the butter, nutmeg and sour cream. Add salt and pepper to taste.

◰ Plum Sauce

It is an old Wiltshire tradition to serve plum sauce with roast lamb or venison. *Makes 2½ cups.*

1 pound firm, ripe plums
1¼ cups white wine vinegar
2 cloves
6 tablespoons sugar
1 tablespoon fresh chopped mint

Wash and pit the plums. Stew them in the vinegar with the cloves and sugar until they are tender. Remove the cloves and puree the mixture in a blender or food processor.

Put the sauce in a saucepan, add the mint and reheat. If you find the sauce is a little too sharp, add more sugar.

⊠ Wow-Wow Sauce

Judging by its name, this sauce must have caused something of a sensation when it first made its appearance in the London chophouses of the early nineteenth century. It has now become associated with Bubble and Squeak, with which it goes very well. *Makes 2 cups.*

1 ounce butter
2 tablespoons flour
1¼ cups Meat Stock
2 tablespoons wine vinegar
1 tablespoon Worcestershire sauce
2 tablespoons prepared English mustard
2 tablespoons chopped parsley
Salt
Freshly ground black pepper
4 pickled walnuts (optional)

Melt the butter in a heavy-bottomed saucepan over low heat. Add the flour and cook for 2 minutes, stirring constantly. Gradually add the Meat Stock and continue to cook until it makes a smooth sauce. Season with vinegar, Worcestershire sauce and mustard and cook gently for an additional 10 minutes. Stir in the parsley and add salt and pepper to taste.

Cut the pickled walnuts into very small pieces and add them to the sauce. Heat thoroughly and serve.

⊠ Hannover Sauce

Serve this sauce with roast chicken, using the liver and giblets to make the sauce. *Makes 2 cups.*

Liver and giblets of 1 chicken
1½ cups water
Juice of ½ a lemon
1 anchovy fillet
1 cup heavy cream
Salt
White pepper

Clean and trim the chicken liver and put it with the giblets in a small saucepan. Add the water and simmer for approximately 20 minutes.

Remove the liver and puree it with the lemon juice, anchovy fillet and cream.

Reheat and season to taste with salt and pepper. Be careful not to oversalt as the anchovy will already have made it quite salty.

⊠ Basic White Sauce

Makes 3 cups.

1½ ounces butter
4 tablespoons flour
3 cups milk
Salt
White pepper

Melt the butter in a heavy-bottomed pan over low heat. Add the flour and cook for about 2 minutes, stirring constantly with a wooden spoon. Gradually pour in the milk, continuing to stir until it is completely absorbed and you have a smooth white sauce. Season to taste with salt and pepper and simmer very gently for 10 to 15 minutes, stirring from time to time.

◙ Parsley Sauce

A delicate-flavored sauce that goes well with any kind of poached whitefish fillets such as flounder or sole. It is also frequently served with smoked haddock. *Makes 3 cups.*

3 cups Basic White Sauce
½ cup Chicken Stock
Juice of 1 lemon
4 tablespoons finely chopped parsley
Salt
White pepper

Prepare Basic White Sauce and add the Chicken Stock, lemon juice and parsley. Reheat the sauce and stir well. Season to taste with salt and pepper.

◙ Anchovy Sauce

Serve this with any kind of poached whitefish. *Makes 3½ cups.*

3 cups Basic White Sauce
2 ounces butter
3 tablespoons anchovy paste
½ cup heavy cream
Salt
Freshly ground black pepper

Prepare the Basic White Sauce. In a separate saucepan melt the butter over low heat. Add the anchovy paste and mix well. Gradually pour in the White Sauce and add the cream. Simmer over low heat for 10 minutes. Season to taste with salt and pepper and serve.

◪ Stilton Sauce

It is customary to serve this sauce with grilled plaice. It is also good with flounder. *Makes 4 cups.*

6 ounces Stilton cheese
3 cups Basic White Sauce
1 cup heavy cream
Salt
Freshly ground black pepper

Crumble the Stilton into small pieces and add them to the White Sauce. Stir the sauce over low heat until the cheese has completely melted. Add the cream and season to taste with salt and pepper.

◪ Gooseberry Sauce

If gooseberries are hard to find, use rhubarb as a substitute. Serve this sauce with grilled mackerel as is traditionally done in Cornwall. The sharp, piquant flavor provides a delicious contrast to the fish. *Makes 3½ cups.*

½ pound gooseberries or rhubarb
3 cups Basic White Sauce
Salt
Freshly ground black pepper

Wash the gooseberries and pinch off their tops and tails. (This is known as topping and tailing.) If you are substituting rhubarb, wash and slice it into 1-inch pieces. Put the fruit in a saucepan with a little water and simmer until it is soft.

Remove the fruit from the pan and puree it in a blender or food processor. (If you are using gooseberries you then need to force them through a sieve so as to eliminate the pips.) Add the fruit to the White Sauce. Season to taste with salt and pepper, reheat and serve.

N.B.: If you are using rhubarb for this recipe, you may want to add 2 or 3 tablespoons of sugar to the puree if it is too tart.

▨ Mustard Sauce

Traditionally, Mustard Sauce is served with grilled herrings. However, try it also with grilled mackerel or with sea bass. *Makes 3 cups.*

1 tablespoon prepared English mustard
1 teaspoon lemon juice
1 teaspoon vinegar
3 cups Basic White Sauce
½ cup heavy cream
Salt
Freshly ground black pepper

Mix the mustard with the lemon juice and vinegar and blend this mixture into the White Sauce.

Heat the sauce over low heat, mix in the cream and allow to simmer for 5 minutes. Season to taste with salt and pepper and serve.

▨ Egg Sauce

A rather unusual sauce that is delicious with any kind of poached or baked whitefish. *Makes 3 cups.*

3 hard-boiled eggs
3 cups Basic White Sauce
Salt
White pepper

Separate the hard-boiled eggs. Chop the whites very fine and rub the yolks through a sieve. Add the whites to the Basic White Sauce. Heat thoroughly over low heat and season to taste with salt and pepper. Just before serving, stir in the sieved yolks.

◪ Onion Sauce

The base of this sauce is a variation of a Basic White Sauce. Instead of being made entirely with milk, some of the liquid in which the onions have been cooked is used to give the sauce an added onion flavor. Serve this sauce with lamb, duck or goose. *Makes 2 cups.*

3 medium-sized onions, peeled
1 bayleaf
¼ teaspoon mace
Salt
1 ounce butter
2 tablespoons flour
1 cup milk
1 teaspoon lemon juice
¼ cup heavy cream

Put the onions in a saucepan and cover them with water. Add the bayleaf, mace and a pinch of salt. Boil covered for 15 minutes or until they are tender.

Remove the onions, drain and set aside. Keep ½ cup of the water in which they were cooked and discard the rest.

Melt the butter in a heavy-bottomed saucepan. Stir in the flour and let it cook for 2 minutes. Gradually add the milk, stirring constantly. When all the milk is absorbed, add the ½ cup of reserved water.

Chop the onions fine and add them to the sauce. Add the lemon juice and cream. Season to taste with salt and simmer for 5 more minutes.

⊠ Basic Brown Sauce

This sauce can be served with ham or veal. It is the base for several other savory sauces. *Makes 3 cups.*

2 ounces butter
2 tablespoons flour
3 cups Meat Stock
¼ cup sherry
½ teaspoon Worcestershire sauce
Salt
Freshly ground black pepper

Melt the butter in a heavy-bottomed saucepan over low heat. Add the flour and cook for 2 minutes, stirring constantly. Gradually add the stock and continue to stir. Finally add the sherry and Worcestershire sauce and season to taste with salt and pepper.

Simmer gently for 10 minutes.

⊠ Caper Sauce

Good with cold roast lamb. *Makes 2 cups.*

2 cups Basic Brown Sauce
½ cup capers
2 tablespoons malt vinegar
Salt
Freshly ground black pepper

Add the capers and vinegar to the Basic Brown Sauce. Heat thoroughly over low heat and season to taste with salt and pepper.

◙ Scrumpy Sauce

In certain parts of Somerset, cider is called "scrumpy," although it is not clear why. Scrumpy or Cider Sauce goes well with ham or venison. *Makes 4½ cups.*

2½ cups apple cider
3 cloves
2 bayleaves
3 cups Basic Brown Sauce
Salt
Freshly ground black pepper

Place the cider, cloves and bayleaves in a saucepan. Bring to a boil and boil vigorously until the liquid is reduced by half. Strain and set aside.

Prepare the Brown Sauce and add the strained cider. Season to taste with salt and pepper, reheat and serve.

◙ Brandy Butter

Brandy Butter, often called Hard Sauce, is traditionally served with Christmas Pudding or Mince Pies. It will keep for several weeks in the refrigerator, so it can be prepared ahead of time. It is extremely rich and a little of it goes a long way. *Makes 2 cups.*

8 ounces softened, unsalted butter
¾ cup dark brown sugar
5 tablespoons brandy
¼ teaspoon nutmeg

Cream the butter and sugar until smooth. Gradually stir in the brandy and add the nutmeg.

Beat thoroughly and transfer to a dish or small pot. Cover and allow to harden before serving.

◩ Cumberland Rum Butter

This makes a nice alternative to <u>Brandy Butter</u> and is frequently served in the north of England. Rum smuggling used to flourish along the shores of Cumberland and local folklore has it that Cumberland Rum Butter was the discovery of an old lady who was storing in her larder an illegal cask of rum that began to leak all over her supplies of sugar and butter! *Makes 2 cups.*

8 ounces softened, unsalted butter
2 cups dark brown sugar
¾ cup rum
¼ teaspoon nutmeg

Cream the butter and sugar until smooth. Gradually stir in the rum and add the nutmeg.

Beat thoroughly and transfer to a dish or a small pot. Allow to harden before serving.

▣ Custard

Custard is terribly British and should be poured lavishly over such puddings as Rhubarb Crumble and Guards' Pudding. It must be served hot and should never be lumpy. *Makes 2 cups.*

1½ cups milk
2 teaspoons cornstarch
1 tablespoon sugar
3 egg yolks
½ teaspoon vanilla extract

In a heavy-bottomed saucepan mix 2 tablespoons of the milk with the cornstarch. As soon as the cornstarch is dissolved, add the rest of the milk and the sugar and cook over moderate heat until the sauce begins to thicken and comes to a boil.

Place the egg yolks in a bowl and beat them with a fork. Take a cup of the sauce and pour it over the eggs, beating as you pour. Return the mixture to the rest of the sauce, stir well and quickly bring back to a boil. Add the vanilla extract, remove from the heat. Pour the custard into a pitcher and serve.

⊠ Jam Sauce

Hot and sticky, this sauce should be served with such steamed puddings as Jam Roly-Poly or Spotted Dick. *Makes about 2 cups.*

½ pound strawberry or raspberry jam
1¼ cups orange juice
1 tablespoon arrowroot
Juice of 1 lemon

Heat the jam and orange juice together in a saucepan and simmer for 5 minutes.

Blend the arrowroot with a little cold water and stir in a few tablespoons of the jam sauce. Pour this mixture into the saucepan with the rest of the jam sauce.

Bring to a boil and stir constantly until the sauce thickens. Add the lemon juice just before serving.

⊠ Melba Sauce

This famous sauce was created by August Escoffier while he was chef at the Savoy Hotel in London, in honor of Dame Nellie Melba, the Australian opera singer, who sang at Covent Garden every year from 1888 to 1926. Escoffier intended that the sauce be poured over vanilla ice cream and served with a poached fresh peach (not a canned one!). It's an irresistible combination, but you might also want to try it with Flummery or any kind of simple milk pudding. *Makes about 2 cups.*

1 pound raspberries, fresh or frozen
Sugar

Rub the raspberries through a sieve to eliminate the pips and sweeten the strained raspberries with sugar to taste.

Savories

■

Angels on Horseback
Scotch Woodcock
Welsh Rarebit
Mushrooms on Toast
Grilled Kidneys
Deviled Chicken Livers
Aberdeen Nips
Locket's Savory
Albany Biscuits
Cheese Straws

The savory is a unique British culinary creation. In the seventeenth and eighteenth centuries, it was the custom at a formal dinner to serve a large selection of dishes, both sweet and savory, at the same time. However, by the nineteenth century, the savory had begun to appear as a separate course, coming at the end of the meal after the sweet course. It served as a transition, and was considered helpful for the digestion since it cleared the palate and, if you were a gentleman, prepared it for the port.

At the beginning of this century, no formal dinner would have been considered complete without a savory. Today the savory has been replaced by cheese. Occasionally, you may find a savory appearing on a dinner menu, although it will usually be offered not in addition to dessert but as an alternative. More often, however, the savory is to be found on the luncheon menu. Since most savories are exactly right for the kind of quick, light lunches that people eat today, a happy transition has been effected and the savory quietly flourishes under a new guise and in a new setting.

▨ Angels on Horseback

Oysters used to be so numerous in England that they had very little value and were eaten mostly by the poor. It is hard to believe, but this Victorian recipe was not considered in any way out of the ordinary. Scallops may be substituted for the oysters, in which case you have Archangels on Horseback. *Serves 6.*

16 large oysters
8 bacon slices, cut in half
4 slices buttered toast, with their crusts removed, cut into
  quarters

Open and clean the oysters. Wrap each one in a slice of bacon and secure it with a small skewer or pin. Put the wrapped oysters in a roasting pan and grill them under a broiler until the bacon is crisp.

Arrange each "angel" on a slice of buttered toast and serve immediately.

◪ Scotch Woodcock

This is really a glorified version of scrambled eggs. In addition to being an agreeable savory, it can hold its own at any brunch. *Serves 4.*

6 eggs
4 tablespoons light cream
Salt
Freshly ground black pepper
3 tablespoons butter
4 slices buttered toast, crusts removed, cut into 8 triangles
2 tablespoons anchovy paste
8 anchovy fillets
1 small bunch watercress

Beat the eggs lightly with a fork in a mixing bowl. Add the cream and a pinch of salt and pepper.

Melt the butter in a heavy-bottomed saucepan over low heat. Pour in the eggs and cook very slowly over low heat, stirring constantly with a wooden spoon. Be careful not to overcook, as the eggs will continue to cook after you have removed them from the heat. Take them off while they are still on the runny side.

Spread the pieces of toast with anchovy paste and arrange on a serving dish. Divide the eggs into equal portions and place on top of the toast. Roll up the anchovy fillets and use one to decorate each portion. Garnish with watercress and serve immediately.

⊠ Welsh Rarebit

Rarebit or rabbit? No one has ever solved this controversy, which dates back to the eighteenth century and still goes on today. Rarebit seems the more likely, but I have seen polemics written on why this is not so. Whatever its correct name, this dish of creamy toasted cheese is probably the best known of all savories. It also makes a wonderful lunch or snack and can be prepared in no time at all. *Serves 6.*

2½ cups grated Cheddar cheese*
1 ounce butter
½ cup ale
2 teaspoons prepared English mustard
Salt
Freshly ground black pepper
6 large slices buttered toast

Melt the cheese and butter in the ale in a small pan. Stir over low heat until the cheese has completely melted.

Add the mustard and a little salt and pepper.

Cut each slice of toast in half and arrange the slices in a shallow ovenproof dish. Pour the cheese mixture over the slices and place under the broiler until the cheese is bubbling and brown.

---

* It is important always to buy Cheddar cut from the wheel. Don't ever use the packaged orange-colored blocks sold in supermarkets under the name Cheddar. Apart from the awful taste, these have been so highly processed that they don't even melt properly.

◻ Mushrooms on Toast

One of the simplest of all savories to prepare and one of the very best. *Serves 6.*

1 tablespoon anchovy paste
4 ounces softened butter
6 large slices toasted white bread
3 cups small button mushrooms, washed and trimmed
Salt
Freshly ground black pepper
2 tablespoons parsley

Mix the anchovy paste with 2 ounces of the butter and spread it on the toast slices. Set aside.

Sauté the mushrooms gently in the remaining butter over low heat for 5 minutes. Season to taste with salt and pepper and arrange them on the toast slices. Decorate with parsley and serve.

◫ Grilled Kidneys

The Victorians loved kidneys as a savory course, and Deviled Kidneys would also have been served frequently as a savory. *Serves 6.*

1 cup breadcrumbs
2 eggs
12 kidneys, cut into small cubes
1 ounce melted butter
Salt
Freshly ground black pepper
6 large slices of hot buttered toast, crusts removed

Put the breadcrumbs in a small bowl. Beat the eggs and put them in another bowl. Dip the kidneys first into the eggs and then into the breadcrumbs.

Thread the kidneys onto skewers, brush with butter and put them under the broiler for 3 to 4 minutes on either side. Sprinkle with salt and pepper and serve on top of the hot buttered toast.

◫ Deviled Chicken Livers

Serves 4.

8 chicken livers
3 scallions, finely chopped
1 teaspoon parsley
½ teaspoon salt
½ teaspoon cayenne pepper
½ teaspoon English mustard
8 bacon slices, cut in half

Cut each chicken liver in half and sprinkle with the scallions, parsley, salt, pepper and mustard.

Wrap each piece of liver in a slice of bacon and fasten with a toothpick. Place under the broiler for a few minutes until cooked and serve immediately.

◪ Aberdeen Nips

A quickly made savory that uses leftover haddock. Another good lunch dish, which should be served with a green salad. *Serves 4.*

1 ounce butter
2 tablespoons flour
2 cups milk
¾ pound cooked smoked haddock
4 egg yolks
Salt
Paprika
4 slices buttered toast, crusts removed
Parsley to garnish

Melt the butter in a saucepan over low heat. Add the flour and cook for about 1 minute or until it begins to bubble. Gradually pour in the milk, stirring constantly.

Remove any skin or bones from the haddock and flake it into small pieces. Add these to the sauce. Beat the egg yolks and add them. Season to taste with the salt and paprika and reheat over low heat.

Pile the mixture onto the slices of buttered toast and place them on a serving dish. Sprinkle each slice with a little paprika and garnish with parsley. Serve immediately.

◧ Locket's Savory

This dish is an old specialty of Locket's restaurant in London.
Serves 4.

1 bunch watercress
4 ripe pears, peeled, cored and cut into thin slices
12 ounces Stilton cheese, cut into slices
Freshly ground black pepper

Cut off the ends of the watercress and lay the rest on the bottom of a shallow, ovenproof dish. Cover with pears and then with the slices of Stilton.

Place the dish in the oven and bake for 10 minutes at 350° until the cheese begins to melt and bubble. Grind black pepper on top and serve.

◫ Albany Biscuits

These savory biscuits are light and crisp. They are particularly good with cheese or Kipper Pâté.

½ cup plus 2 tablespoons milk
1 ounce butter
1¾ cups flour
Salt

Preheat the oven to 400°.

Put the milk and butter in a saucepan over low heat until the butter is melted.

Sift the flour and a pinch of salt into a bowl and pour the milky butter into it gradually. Stir well until the mixture becomes a soft dough. Roll out very thin on a well-floured board and cut into rounds of approximately 2½ inches, using a glass or a cookie cutter.

Prick each round several times with a fork and put it pricked side down on a well-greased baking tray.

Bake for 5 minutes, then turn and bake for another 5 minutes. The biscuits should be lightly colored but not brown. Cool on a wire rack and store in an airtight container.

◩ Cheese Straws

2 cups flour
Salt
Freshly ground black pepper
4 ounces butter
1 beaten egg
1–2 tablespoons water
1½ cups grated sharp Cheddar cheese
½ cup grated Parmesan cheese
Paprika

Sift the flour together with a pinch of salt and pepper into a mixing bowl. Rub in the butter until the mixture resembles coarse breadcrumbs. Stir in the beaten egg, 1 tablespoon of water and the cheese. Mix to a rough dough. If the dough seems too dry, add the other tablespoon of water.

Roll the dough into a ball, wrap it in waxed paper and store in the refrigerator for half an hour.

Preheat the oven to 400°.

Roll out the dough in the shape of a rectangle on a lightly floured surface. It should be about 1 inch thick.

Using a pastry cutter or a sharp knife, cut the pastry into sticks ½-inch thick and 4 inches long. Place the strips on 2 large baking sheets and bake in the oven for 8 to 10 minutes or until the sticks are a pale golden color.

Transfer the cheese straws to a wire rack. When they have cooled slightly, dip the ends in a little paprika and serve while they are still warm.

Puddings
and
Desserts

Sussex Pond Pudding
Spotted Dick
Jam Roly-Poly
Mrs. Messenger's Christmas Plum Pudding
Guards' Pudding
Treacle Sponge Pudding
Apple Charlotte
Apple Cinnamon
Queen of Puddings
Sister Agatha's Rhubarb Crumble
Baked Almond Pudding
Bread and Butter Pudding
Rice Pudding
West Riding Pudding
Treacle Tart
Bakewell Tart
Pancakes
Apple Fritters
Poor Knights of Windsor
Summer Pudding
Trifle
Nanny Merriman's Basic Lemon Fluff
Buttered Oranges
Burnt Cream
Eton Mess
Floating Islands
Syllabub
Gooseberry Fool
Flummery
Port Jelly
Old English Rhubarb Jelly
Brown Bread Ice Cream
Tea Ice Cream

*Blessed be he that invented pudding, for it is a manna
that hits the palates of all sorts of people.*
—François Misson, a Protestant exile who came to
England at the end of the seventeenth century

English puddings have a deservedly great reputation, and the proverbial English sweet tooth is almost a national characteristic.

Actually, the earliest English puddings weren't sweet at all. They started out as savory puddings such as bacon badger pudding, offal pudding, cow-heel pudding and partridge pudding and were cooked in a bag made from the stomach of an animal. Later they were cooked in a piece of cloth or in a bowl with a suet crust, but they continued to be savory puddings until the middle of the seventeenth century when sugar became less expensive and almonds, raisins and dried fruit began to be used as ingredients.

Sweet puddings have been in fashion since the time of George I. He adored them rich and heavy and was known to all his subjects as "the pudding king." Although personally unpopular for his German manners and his inability to speak English, he did a great deal to establish the sweet pudding as an integral part of his new country's cuisine. It soon became something of a national institution and in 1726 John Arbuthnot, court physician to Queen Anne, declared, "Let not Englishmen therefore be asham'd of the Name of 'Pudding-Eaters.' " Soon, every town, every profession, every great occasion and even every battle boasted its own pudding. Mrs. Beeton offered her readers over 200 pudding recipes and in 1910, Cassell's *Shilling Cookery* "responding to public demand" came out with 370 recipes.

The term "pudding" is a little confusing since most Americans think of pudding as a thick, soft dessert. However, in Britain pudding not only refers to steamed puddings, baked puddings, pies, tarts, creams, trifles, jellies, fools and milk puddings; it has become synonymous with the word dessert. (I have a clear memory of my great aunt, at the conclusion of a marvelous lunch, asking a guest if he would care for pudding and then proceeding to offer him an orange. The guest, who happened to be American but thought he understood all things English, was distinctly puzzled.)

Puddings owe a great deal to Nanny, who considered that no meal was complete without one and no pudding was complete without custard. Perhaps she liked puddings for themselves, but they were also part of her elaborate reward system: No vegetable, no pudding. Thanks to her influence, generations of English children have grown up with nostalgic memories of such delights as Spotted Dick, Floating Islands, Jam Roly-Poly and Bread and Butter Pudding, and what Englishman, when confronted with an enticing choice of sophisticated desserts, will not happily pick out his old nursery favorite, smothered in Custard. However, not all childhood pudding memories are idyllic. Scratch the surface, and you may be given gory descriptions of such school horrors as Boiled Baby, Wet Nelly, Dead Man's Leg and Washerwoman's Arm (all nicknames for poorly made steamed puddings).

Today, puddings have shrunk in importance somewhat and their appearance at every lunch and dinner, while still desirable, is no longer considered obligatory. This is due partly to the fact that we tend to eat less today and partly to the proliferation of instant mixes, packages and powders that have given puddings a bad name. However, although there must be few British housewives who still make a different pudding every day, there is a growing interest in rediscovering the traditional country puddings so loved by our grandparents, and more and more cooks are learning the delights of a steaming Sussex Pond Pudding, a crisp Treacle Tart, a smooth white Flummery or a succulent Burnt Cream.

◪ Sussex Pond Pudding

Be sure to try this recipe. It is one of the oldest and most original of all suet puddings. A whole lemon mixed with brown sugar and butter and cooked in a pastry case results in a marmaladelike juice that spills out when the pudding is sliced to make a moat or pond around the pastry. Keep Sussex Pond for special occasions and serve it with lots of heavy cream. *Serves 6.*

2 cups flour
2 teaspoons baking powder
1 cup shredded suet
Approximately 1 cup of equal amounts of milk and water
1 large lemon
4 ounces butter, cut into small pieces
¾ cup dark brown sugar

Place the flour, baking powder and suet in a bowl and mix them together well. Add enough of the milk/water liquid to make a fairly soft dough. Roll it out in a round shape large enough to line a pudding bowl that holds approximately 5 cups or an earthenware or Pyrex bowl. Be sure that the container is well greased.

Cut off ¼ of the pastry round and set it aside to use for the pastry lid. Place the rest of the pastry in the bowl, stretching it with your fingers to make sure it reaches all around the top and that there are no cracks where the sides join.

Prick the lemon lavishly with a darning needle and place it in the bowl. Surround it with the butter and sugar. Roll out the remaining pastry so that it fits the top of the bowl and press the edges well down. Trim with a knife and place a large piece of aluminum foil over the pudding. Make a pleat in the center and tuck it around the sides of the basin. Tie it in place under the rim with a piece of string.

Place the bowl on a steamer rack or an inverted saucer in a large saucepan half filled with boiling water. Cover and boil for 3½ hours, adding water if the level should begin to sink.

TO SERVE: Remove the bowl from the saucepan and take off

the foil. Ease the pudding gently with a knife and turn it onto a serving plate. Cut the pudding as if it were a cake and make sure everyone gets a piece of the lemon.

◪ Spotted Dick

Spotted Dick, sometimes also known as Spotted Dog, is a simple, uncomplicated steamed pudding "spotted" with raisins and currants that is much beloved by large numbers of serious pudding eaters. Serve with Custard. *Serves 4–6.*

1 cup flour
1 cup shredded suet
1 cup freshly made breadcrumbs
¾ cup raisins
¾ cup currants
5 tablespoons sugar
Pinch of salt
½ teaspoon mixed spice
½ cup plus 2 tablespoons milk

Mix all the dry ingredients together and add the milk to make a dough. Butter a pudding bowl that holds approximately 5 cups and put the dough in it.

Cover the top of the bowl with a large piece of aluminum foil. Make a pleat in the center and tie it in place around the rim with string. Put the bowl on a steamer rack or an inverted saucer in a large saucepan in approximately 3 inches of water, cover and steam for 2½ hours. Check the level of the water from time to time, and add more if necessary.

TO SERVE: Remove the foil and run a knife gently around the pudding. Turn onto a serving plate and serve hot.

⊠ Jam Roly-Poly

An old-fashioned English nursery suet pudding that is warm, filling, fattening and quite delicious! It looks very similar to a jelly roll, but it is steamed, not cooked in an oven. Serve with Jam Sauce or Custard. *Serves 6.*

1½ cups flour
1½ teaspoons baking powder
Salt
¾ cup shredded suet
Approximately ¾ cup of equal amounts of milk and water
1 cup raspberry or strawberry jam

Mix the flour, baking powder and a pinch of salt with the suet in a mixing bowl. Stir in enough of the milk/water liquid to make a stiff dough.

Form the dough into a ball and roll it out in the shape of a rectangle on a well-floured surface. It should be approximately 10 inches long and 4 inches wide. Moisten the edges with a little water.

Spread the jam over the pastry, keeping it away from the edges.

Roll the pastry round and round so that it looks like a long log and try not to let any of the jam seep out. Press the edges tightly together and wrap the Roly-Poly in aluminum foil. Make 2 or 3 pleats in the foil so that the pudding has room to expand and tie both ends with a piece of string.

Fill a large saucepan half full of boiling water and place the Roly-Poly in it. Cover and boil for 2 hours, adding water if necessary to keep the pan half full.

Remove the pudding from the saucepan and allow it to cool slightly before unwrapping the foil. Slide the Roly-Poly onto a plate and serve.

◙ Mrs. Messenger's Christmas Plum Pudding

According to Mrs. Beeton, Plum Pudding "is seasonable on December 25th and on various festive occasions until March." She is absolutely right—Plum Pudding is far too good to be eaten only on Christmas Day, and most British cooks make 2 or 3 puddings at the same time. With this recipe you can either make 1 large pudding or 2 smaller ones. Remember to prepare your pudding(s) at least 3 months beforehand; some cooks like to make their puddings up to a year ahead of time. Everybody has his own favorite recipe for Plum Pudding. This one, which is not hard to prepare, comes from my cousin's mother-in-law. Serve with Brandy Butter. *Serves 8.*

1 cup currants
1 cup white raisins
1½ cups raisins
1 cup flour
2 cups stale breadcrumbs
1 cup shredded suet
1 cup plus 2 tablespoons dark brown sugar
¼ cup chopped almonds
4 beaten eggs
2 tablespoons Guinness
Juice of 1 lemon
Juice of 1 orange
½ teaspoon allspice
1 teaspoon nutmeg
½ cup rum
2 tablespoons candied fruit peel

Mix all the ingredients together in a large bowl and put them in either 1 English pudding bowl that holds approximately 7–8 cups or 2 smaller bowls if you prefer to make 2 puddings. Leave at least 1 inch at the top of the bowl so that the pudding has room to expand.

Cover with two sheets of waxed paper and a layer of aluminum foil. Tie the top tightly around the rim of the basin with string and make a handle so that the pudding can be lifted.

Place an upturned saucer in the bottom of a large pan of water and bring the water to a boil. Lower the pudding bowl into the water so that it stands on the saucer and make sure that the water comes at least ¾ of the way up. Cover and boil over low heat for 7 hours, checking from time to time to make sure that the water level does not drop. If it does, add more water.

Remove the pudding from the water and store it in a cool place.

On the day you eat the pudding, you should boil it for 2 hours in the same way as before. Then remove the cover and turn the pudding onto a serving plate.

Before serving, warm a little brandy in a saucepan, pour it over the top of the pudding and light it with a match.

◪ Guards' Pudding

Unexpectedly dark, heavy and sweet, Guards' Pudding is one of my favorites of all steamed puddings. It tastes rather like a Christmas pudding without the fruit. Serve with <u>Custard</u>. *Serves 4–6.*

4 ounces butter
8 tablespoons dark brown sugar
3 tablespoons raspberry or strawberry jam
1 teaspoon baking soda
1 cup fresh breadcrumbs, made from brown or whole-wheat
  bread
2 eggs
Salt

Cream the butter and sugar and blend in the jam. Dissolve the baking soda in a little warm water. Add the breadcrumbs, eggs, a pinch of salt and the baking soda to the jam mixture and mix together. Place all the ingredients in a well-greased pudding bowl that holds approximately 5 cups.

Cover the top with a large piece of aluminum foil that has been pleated down the middle. Fasten it around the rim of the basin with either string or a rubber band. Place the bowl in a large saucepan or steamer in 3 inches of water. The bowl should stand on a steamer rack or an inverted saucer.

Cover and steam for 2 hours, checking from time to time to make sure the water has not evaporated. If necessary, add more water.

TO SERVE: Remove the bowl from the steamer and take off the foil cover. Run a knife gently around the edge of the bowl and turn the pudding onto a serving dish. Serve hot.

◪ Treacle Sponge Pudding

This rich sponge pudding, which has its own syrup sauce, resembles a steamed pudding although it is actually cooked in the oven. This makes it much quicker to prepare and also gives it a certain lightness. Children love it!

4 ounces softened butter
½ cup plus 2 tablespoons sugar
2 eggs
Grated rind of 1 lemon
1¼ cups flour
1 teaspoon baking powder
Pinch of salt
2 teaspoons milk
4 tablespoons dark corn syrup
SAUCE:
4 tablespoons dark corn syrup
2 tablespoons water
Juice of 1 lemon

Preheat the oven to 400°.

Cream the butter and sugar in a bowl until soft and fluffy. Add the eggs and lemon rind and fold in the flour, baking powder and salt. Add the milk last.

Grease a pudding bowl that holds approximately 3 cups and pour 4 tablespoons of corn syrup over the bottom. Put the sponge mixture on top. Cover with a loose-fitting sheet of aluminum foil and place in an ovenproof dish or pan in 1 inch of water.

Cook in the oven for 45 minutes or until the sponge has set and the top has turned a light golden color. (Use a toothpick to test for setting.)

Turn the pudding onto a serving dish, being sure to scrape out all the syrup at the bottom of the basin. Heat the remaining corn syrup, water and lemon juice in a double boiler for approximately 5 minutes, pour it over the top of the pudding, and serve.

◪ Apple Charlotte

Apple Charlotte, also known as Brown Betty, is another of those simple, fattening, irresistible British puddings. *Serves 4–6.*

1 cup dark brown sugar
½ teaspoon cinnamon
10–12 slices whole-wheat bread, buttered and with the
  crusts removed
2 pounds apples, peeled, cored and sliced
5 tablespoons dark corn syrup

Preheat the oven to 350°.

Grease a deep 9-inch-wide pie dish and coat it with 1½ tablespoons of the brown sugar mixed with a little of the cinnamon.

Line the dish with the bread slices, buttered side up. (Set aside enough slices to cover the top of the dish.)

Put the apples in layers on the bread in the dish. Sprinkle each layer with a dash of cinnamon and a tablespoon of brown sugar. Cover the top with the reserved bread slices and dredge with the remaining brown sugar.

Pour the syrup over the bread and bake for 30 minutes.

◨ Apple Cinnamon

Since this pudding is really an apple cake, it makes a substantial dessert and is a good way to conclude a light meal. *Serves 6.*

2 eggs
1¼ cups sugar
⅓ cup light cream
4 ounces butter
1¾ cups flour
1½ teaspoons baking powder
1 teaspoon cinnamon
4 medium-sized apples, peeled, cored and sliced

Preheat the oven to 400°.

Beat the eggs and 1 cup of the sugar in a good-sized mixing bowl. Bring the cream and butter to just below the boiling point over low heat. Remove and pour onto the egg and sugar mixture; fold in the flour, baking powder and cinnamon.

Grease a square 9 inch by 9 inch baking pan. Pour in the mixture and arrange the apples on top. Cover with the remaining sugar and bake for about 20 minutes, or until the pudding is firm to the touch.

Serve warm directly from the pan.

◨ Queen of Puddings

Although this pudding has humble nursery origins, it is rightly called a queen of puddings and won't let you down on even the most formal occasion. It consists of a delicate custard punctuated with raspberry jam and topped with a layer of meringue. Serve hot or cold with cream. *Serves 6.*

1¾ cups fresh white breadcrumbs
Grated peel of 1 lemon
1 heaping tablespoon sugar
2 cups milk
3 ounces softened butter
4 egg yolks
½ teaspoon vanilla extract
3 tablespoons raspberry jam
MERINGUE TOPPING:
4 egg whites
⅔ cup sugar

Preheat the oven to 350°.

Put the breadcrumbs, lemon peel and sugar into a mixing bowl. Bring the milk and butter to just below the boiling point over medium heat. Pour them on top of the breadcrumb mixture and allow to stand for 5 minutes.

Beat the egg yolks and vanilla extract and stir them into the breadcrumb mixture.

Grease a round 9-inch soufflé dish and pour in the mixture. Bake for approximately 25 minutes, or until the pudding is firm to the touch.

Remove the pudding from the oven and set aside to cool for 5 minutes. Spread the jam on top.

Beat the egg whites until they are stiff. Add half the sugar and continue beating until they form firm peaks. Fold in the remaining sugar with a metal spoon and pile on top of the pudding.

Return the pudding to the oven and cook for an additional 15 minutes, or until the meringue is slightly brown.

◨ Sister Agatha's Rhubarb Crumble

In my final year at boarding school, a weekly cookery class was part of the curriculum. I don't remember much about what we learned, although I do recollect that nothing ever seemed to turn out the way it was intended. However, our teacher, Sister Agatha, came through with one winning recipe—her crumble was a sensation and is still one of my favorite desserts. Its secret lies in the generous proportions of butter and sugar. Its charm is that it is very straightforward to prepare and virtually foolproof. Serve with whipped cream or <u>Custard</u>. *Serves 6.*

1½ cups flour
1½ cups dark brown sugar
6 ounces butter, cut into small pieces
1 pound rhubarb, washed and cut into 1-inch cubes
2 tablespoons lemon juice
½ cup sugar
½ teaspoon cinnamon

Preheat the oven to 300°.

Put the flour and brown sugar in a mixing bowl. Add the butter and rub it in with your fingers until the mixture resembles coarse breadcrumbs.

Put the rhubarb in a pie or soufflé dish and sprinkle it with the lemon juice, sugar and cinnamon. Heap the crumble mixture on top, pressing it down gently; make sure that all the rhubarb is covered.

Bake in the oven for 20 minutes or until the crumble is golden and the rhubarb is beginning to bubble up around the edges.

Serve hot or cold.

N.B.: Crumble is also delicious made with plums, apples or apricots. If you substitute any of these fruits, use slightly less sugar and slightly more lemon juice.

◙ Baked Almond Pudding

This pudding, which has a cakelike outside and a soft center, should be served hot. It is very good, especially if you are fond of almonds. Serve with cream. *Serves 4–6.*

3 ounces butter
½ cup ground almonds
4 drops almond essence
3 beaten eggs
Rind and juice of ½ lemon
¼ cup sweet sherry
½ cup sugar
1½ cups heavy cream

Preheat the oven to 375°.

Melt the butter in a small saucepan. Remove it from the heat and stir in the remaining ingredients. Turn the mixture into a well-greased pie dish or ovenproof soufflé dish.

Bake for approximately 45 minutes and test with a knife to see if the pudding is cooked. The outside should be firm and the center still runny.

◪ Bread and Butter Pudding

No doubt this recipe was invented to use up the endless slices of bread and butter left over from every Victorian tea table. However, don't let an oversupply of bread be your only excuse for making this dessert. For an interesting variation, use slices of brown bread and spread them with marmalade as well as butter. Serve with cream. *Serves 6.*

3 cups milk
Grated rind of 1 lemon
2 tablespoons sugar
4 slices white bread, crusts removed, spread with butter
½ cup raisins
3 eggs
1 tablespoon brandy
¼ teaspoon grated nutmeg
1 tablespoon dark brown sugar

Heat the milk with the lemon rind and sugar in a small saucepan, and when it reaches the simmering point, set it aside and allow the milk to infuse the lemon peel for at least 10 minutes.

Butter a 1½-pint pie dish. Cut the bread slices in half and place them in layers in the dish, sprinkling the raisins between layers.

Beat the eggs, add the brandy and pour into the milk. Pour the whole mixture over the bread and allow to soak for ½ hour.

Sprinkle the nutmeg and brown sugar over the top of the pudding and bake at 325° for 45 minutes, or until the top is golden.

▧ Rice Pudding

What is the matter with Mary Jane?
It's lovely rice pudding for dinner again!

With these lines, A. A. Milne immortalized another unfortunate recipe, all but ruined through its long association with institutional kitchens. Although it is often uninspiring, there is no reason why Rice Pudding cannot taste superb. The secret is to cook it very slowly so that it has time to form a thick, rich brown skin. Serve with cream and fresh fruit. *Serves 4.*

½ cup short-grain rice
3 cups milk
Pinch of salt
5 tablespoons sugar
¼ teaspoon vanilla essence
½ ounce butter
¼ teaspoon grated nutmeg

Preheat the oven to 275°.

Butter a 1-quart pie or soufflé dish. Wash the rice and put it in the bottom of the dish.

Heat the milk, salt, sugar and vanilla in a saucepan, stirring well to dissolve the sugar. When the mixture begins to simmer, remove it from the heat. Pour it over the rice, dot with tiny pieces of butter and sprinkle the nutmeg over the top.

Set the dish in the oven and cook it for 2½ hours. During the first hour of cooking time, stir the pudding occasionally until the rice gets soft and the milk becomes creamy.

Serve warm.

◪ West Riding Pudding

One of the things I most dislike about cooking is that I always seem to have leftover egg whites lurking reproachfully at the back of the refrigerator. I am particularly fond of this recipe, not only because it gets rid of those dreaded egg whites but because its other ingredients are so basic that one tends to have them all on hand. Best of all, West Riding Pudding—essentially a light sponge with a hint of raspberry jam and a meringue topping—is invariably well received. Serve with cream or Custard. *Serves 4.*

1 cup sugar
4 ounces butter
1 cup flour
1¼ teaspoons baking powder
2 eggs
4 tablespoons raspberry jam
Meringue (see Queen of Puddings)

Preheat the oven to 300°.

Cream the sugar and butter. Sift the flour and baking powder together and add them to the creamed sugar and butter. Mix thoroughly. Beat the eggs and add them to the mixture.

Grease a pie or soufflé dish and spread the raspberry jam over the bottom. Pour the egg mixture over the jam and bake in the oven for approximately 45 minutes or until the sponge has risen and is set. Remove and set aside.

Prepare the meringue and pile it on top of the pudding. Reduce the oven temperature to 250° and cook for a further 15 minutes, or until the meringue has set and is slightly browned.

Serve hot or cold.

◼ Treacle Tart

Treacle tart, an open-faced pie with a filling made of treacle and breadcrumbs (molasses can be substituted for treacle), is customarily served for Sunday dinner, following Roast Beef and Yorkshire Pudding. Serve with whipped cream. *Serves 4–6.*

Shortcrust Pastry
2 cups molasses
1½ cups fresh white breadcrumbs
1 teaspoon lemon juice
1 egg, beaten with a teaspoon of water

Use two thirds of the Shortcrust Pastry to line a 9-inch pie pan. Crimp the edges with a fork.

Mix the syrup, breadcrumbs and lemon juice and spread them over the pastry. Roll out the remaining pastry, cut it into ¼-inch strips and form a lattice top over the filling. Brush the pastry with the egg and water mixture and bake at 350° for 10 minutes. Reduce the heat to 300° and bake for another 20 to 25 minutes, or until the filling is lightly set.

Serve hot.

◪ Bakewell Tart

The story goes that the first Bakewell Tart was the result of a misunderstanding between Mrs. Greaves, the proprietress of the Rutford Arms Inn at Bakewell, and her cook. Mrs. Greaves requested a jam custard tart. However, instead of mixing in the jam with the custard, her cook spread it on the bottom separately. The incorrect tart was an instant success with Mrs. Greaves's guests and has been famous ever since. Bakewell Tart or Bakewell Pudding, as it is sometimes called, is still made in the village of Bakewell in Derbyshire. Serve with whipped cream. *Serves 6.*

Shortcrust Pastry
4 tablespoons strawberry jam
4 eggs
8 tablespoons sugar
4 ounces butter
¾ cup ground almonds

Preheat the oven to 350°.

Roll out the pastry and line a 9-inch pie pan. Spread the jam over the pastry and set aside.

Beat the eggs and sugar together. Melt the butter in a small saucepan and when it is melted and beginning to brown, add it to the egg and sugar mixture. Fold in the almonds and place the mixture over the strawberry jam.

Bake until set (allow 20–25 minutes) and serve hot or cold.

⊠ Pancakes

English Pancakes are a little different from their American counterparts. They are very thin and are served either rolled up with lemon and sugar sprinkled on top, or flat and piled on top of each other. The latter method is called a "Quire of Paper." Pancakes are traditional fare for Shrove Tuesday, a custom that dates back to the Middle Ages when every household had to use up all its eggs and milk before the beginning of Lent.

The town of Olney in Buckinghamshire still holds an annual Shrove Tuesday pancake race and any woman over 16 years old wearing a skirt and apron is eligible to take part. The race is believed to have originated in the fifteenth century when an Olney housewife, hearing the church bell, became so nervous she would be late for the service that she ran out of the house carrying her frying pan and tossing her last pancake. The local church bell is now known as the Pancake Bell, and it is rung at the beginning of the race. The rules require that the successful contestant must toss her pancake at least three times during the course of the race. The finishing point is the church porch, the local vicar is the judge and the prize is a prayer book! *Serves 6.*

1¾ cups flour
Salt
2 teaspoons sugar
2 eggs
1 egg yolk
1 cup milk
1 cup water
Grated rind of ½ lemon
3 teaspoons melted butter
Oil for frying
Juice of 1 lemon
Sugar for sprinkling

Sift the flour with a good pinch of salt and the sugar. Beat the eggs and egg yolk and add them slowly to the flour. Add the milk and water and beat until the batter is covered with bubbles. Add the lemon rind and let the batter stand in a cool place for at least 1 hour.

Stir the melted butter into the pancake batter.

Heat a little oil in a medium-sized pan and when it is very hot begin to cook the pancakes, using a small amount of batter for each pancake so that it is very thin. Flip the pancake once.

As soon as a pancake is cooked and you have removed it from the pan, sprinkle it with lemon juice and sugar.

⊠ Apple Fritters

Apple Fritters, a variation of Pancakes, must be eaten very hot. Prepare the batter and apples ahead of time but don't make the fritters until the very last moment. *Serves 6.*

4 large apples, cored, peeled and cut into ¼-inch slices
2 teaspoons confectioners' sugar
1 cup flour
2 eggs
1 cup Guinness
2 tablespoons sugar
½ teaspoon grated nutmeg
2 teaspoons melted butter
Oil
Sugar

Dust the apple slices with the confectioners' sugar and set aside.

Place the flour in a bowl; make a well in the center and beat in the eggs. Gradually add the Guinness and continue to beat until the mixture has the consistency of heavy cream. Add the sugar and nutmeg and allow the batter to stand for at least 1 hour.

Add the melted butter to the batter and heat a little oil in a medium-sized frying pan. Dip the apple slices in the batter and fry them on both sides until they are golden brown.

Drain them on paper towels and serve sprinkled with sugar.

◨ Poor Knights of Windsor

I have never found out the origin of this recipe or where its name comes from. However, it is particularly pleasant because of the contrast between the hot toasted bread (which is similar to French toast) and the cold raspberries and cream. *Serves 4–6.*

2 cups raspberries
3 tablespoons confectioners' sugar
1 cup heavy cream
½ cup sherry
3 egg yolks, lightly beaten
6–8 slices bread, crusts removed, cut in triangles
3 ounces butter
1 teaspoon cinnamon

Sprinkle the raspberries with confectioners' sugar, crush them gently with a fork and set aside.

Whip the cream until it is stiff.

Place the sherry in one bowl and the lightly beaten egg yolks in another. Dip the bread slices first in the sherry and then in the egg yolks.

Melt the butter in a frying pan and when it is hot, fry the bread on both sides until it is golden brown. Transfer the slices to a warm dish and sprinkle each slice with a little cinnamon.

Place a few of the raspberries on each slice of the toasted bread and cover with a dollop of cream.

Serve immediately.

⊠ Summer Pudding

Summer Pudding, which used to be known as Hydropathic Pudding, was an eighteenth-century invention expressly created for those who could not tolerate the rich pastry desserts so fashionable at the time. It turns out to be one of the very best of all English puddings and should be served with lots of whipped cream. *Serves 6.*

3 pounds mixed berries (use any combination of raspberries,
*   blueberries, cranberries or red currants)*
1 cup sugar (increase this amount to 2 cups if you use a lot of
*   red currants or cranberries)*
8–10 slices good white bread, with crusts removed

Wash and rinse the fruit and remove any stems, leaves, and so forth. Put in a saucepan, add the sugar and cook over low heat, stirring frequently until the sugar has dissolved.

Grease a 1-quart pudding bowl and line the bottom and sides with all but 3 slices of the bread. Make sure that there are no gaps between the seams—trim the slices so that they fit together exactly.

Pour the fruit mixture into the bowl over the bread and cover the top with the remaining slices of bread, which should also be fitted together so that there are no cracks.

Cover the top of the bowl with a flat plate that fits neatly inside the rim and put a heavy weight on top of the plate. If you do not have such an object, an unopened can may be substituted. Refrigerate overnight.

Before serving, remove the plate and run a knife gently around the inside of the bowl. Turn the pudding onto a serving dish. The fruit will have completely saturated the bread and it will be a wonderful dark purple color.

▧ Trifle

Trifle, a favorite Victorian recipe, is the perfect party dessert. Make it well ahead of time, so that the sherry and brandy have enough time to seep into the cake. The charm of Trifle lies in its different textures. Since these also look interesting, Trifle should be served in a glass bowl so that the effect can be seen to full advantage. As an alternative, serve it in individual glass dishes. *Serves 6–8.*

1 leftover Sponge or Madeira Cake (approximately ¾ pound)
1 cup raspberry jam
¼ cup slivered almonds
¼ cup brandy
¾ cup sherry
1½ cups milk
1 cup heavy cream
1 vanilla pod
1 teaspoon cornstarch
3 tablespoons sugar
5 eggs
2 cups whipped heavy cream
8 citron slices
6 crystallized violets or fresh strawberries

Cut the cake into very thick slices and spread each slice with a generous amount of raspberry jam. Arrange the slices on the bottom of a large glass bowl. If you prefer to use individual glass dishes, divide the cake equally among the dishes. Sprinkle the almonds over the cake slices, pour on the brandy and sherry and allow to soak for about 45 minutes (but not longer or the cake will become too soggy).

Bring the milk and cream with the vanilla pod to a boil in a double boiler. Remove from the heat and discard the vanilla pod.

Mix the cornstarch with the sugar and eggs and gradually pour in the milk and cream. Transfer the mixture back to the double boiler and stir until the custard becomes thick and creamy. Do not allow to boil.

Let the custard cool a little and then pour it over the cake. Let the trifle set and when it is fully cooled, spread any remaining raspberry jam on top, then cover with whipped cream.

Decorate the trifle with the citron slices and crystallized violets or strawberries and refrigerate until ready to serve.

◪ Nanny Merriman's Basic Lemon Fluff

This pudding, really a simplified mousse, was invented by a London nanny during the post–World War II rationing period, when eggs were available but cream was still difficult to find. The recipe has been passed from family to family and has long outlived both Nanny Merriman and the days of rationing. *Serves 6.*

3 eggs, separated
¾ cup sugar
Juice of 1 large lemon
Grated peel of 1 lemon
2 envelopes unflavored gelatin (2 tablespoons)
2 small cans evaporated milk (5.33 fl. oz. each)
Confectioners' sugar
8 crystallized violets

Mix the egg yolks and the sugar in the top of a double boiler over low heat. Add the lemon juice and grated peel.

Dissolve the gelatin in 2 tablespoons of boiling water and add it to the egg and lemon mixture. Remove the saucepan from the heat and set it aside.

Beat the evaporated milk in a bowl until it is double its original bulk and add the egg mixture to it.

Beat the egg whites until stiff and fold them into the milk-and-egg mixture. Transfer to a soufflé dish and refrigerate for at least 2 hours.

Before serving, dust with confectioners' sugar and decorate with the crystallized violets.

◻ Buttered Oranges

A recipe for Buttered Oranges can be found in Ann Blencowe's cookery book published in 1694; they are also sometimes referred to as Nell Gwynn's Buttered Oranges, as she was believed to have served them to Charles II.

Buttered Oranges are delicious, and they look spectacular. *Serves 4.*

5 large juicy oranges
4 tablespoons sugar
6 egg yolks
2 tablespoons sherry
1 teaspoon rosewater (optional)
4 ounces butter
1 cup heavy cream
Crystallized violets for decoration (optional)

TO PREPARE THE ORANGE SHELLS: Hold the orange so that the stalk is at the base and using a small knife cut off the top about two inches down. Scoop out all the flesh, being careful not to break the skin. This can be done quite easily with a teaspoon. Using a pair of scissors, cut off the stalk that remains in the bottom, wash the orange and set it aside (the top can be discarded). Repeat this procedure with three more of the oranges.

Grate the peel off the remaining orange and then squeeze all the juice from this orange into a bowl. Place the flesh you have extracted from the other oranges in a sieve and squeeze all the juice into the same bowl.

Mix the juice with the sugar and egg yolks in a double boiler over low heat. Beat with a wire whisk until the mixture begins to thicken. Remove the top of the double boiler and cool it in a bowl of cold water while you continue to stir; then add the sherry and rosewater.

Remove the bowl from the cold water. Cut the butter into 1-inch cubes and mash it into the mixture piece by piece. Add the orange peel.

Whip ¾ of the cream and fold it into the mixture. Pour the mixture into the four orange shells and refrigerate for at least 2 hours.

Before serving, place three crystallized violets on the top of each orange; whip the remaining cream and force it through a pastry tube in a curly pattern around the top edges.

⊠ Burnt Cream

Burnt Cream, sometimes known as Trinity Cream since it is generally believed to have originated at Trinity College, Cambridge, in the eighteenth century, is the English relation (and predecessor) of the French Crème Brûlée. *Serves 4–6.*

5 egg yolks
1 cup plus 2 tablespoons sugar
2 cups heavy cream
2 drops vanilla essence or a 2-inch vanilla pod

Beat the yolks with 2 tablespoons of the sugar for at least 3 minutes in an electric beater or food processor, or for 10 minutes by hand. Add the cream and continue to beat well until the mixture is thick and creamy. Transfer to a saucepan and add the vanilla. Bring the mixture gently to just below the boiling point, stirring constantly. Do not allow it to boil or it will curdle. If you are using a vanilla pod, remove it at this time. Pour the mixture into a shallow ovenproof dish and allow it to cool to room temperature, then refrigerate for at least 2 hours until it has thickened.

Just before serving, put the dish in the freezer for 10 minutes, then sprinkle the remaining sugar over the top and place the dish under a very hot broiler so that the sugar caramelizes to a deep glaze.

◩ Eton Mess

Eton, probably the best known of all English public schools, is famous for its playing fields (large), wing collars (stiff), boating song (a rousing tune) and a recipe known as Eton Mess (delicious)! What most likely began as strawberries and cream and is traditionally eaten on the fourth of June—the annual prizegiving day when parents and students picnic together on the illustrious playing fields—has evolved over the years into a glorious concoction of strawberries soaked in kirsch and mixed with crushed meringues and lots of whipped cream.

You may want to make the meringues ahead of time. If you do, be sure to store them in an airtight container or they will lose their crispness. *Serves 4–6.*

1 pound strawberries, washed and hulled
5 tablespoons kirsch
2 cups heavy cream
MERINGUES:
3 egg whites
Pinch of salt
12 tablespoons sugar

Set aside 6 of the strawberries. Cut the rest in half, put them in a shallow bowl and sprinkle the kirsch over them. Chill for at least 2 hours.

TO PREPARE THE MERINGUES: Beat the egg whites until they are very stiff and then add the salt. Fold in the sugar by hand, using a metal spoon.

Spoon onto a well-greased baking tray in mounds that are about 3 inches in diameter.

Bake at 200° for 2 hours. Turn off the oven and open the oven door. Do not remove the meringues until the oven has fully cooled.

Whip the cream until it is stiff.

Just before serving, break the meringues into small pieces and mix them with the strawberries. Mix the whipped cream with the meringues and the strawberries. Turn the mixture into a glass bowl. Decorate with the six whole strawberries and serve.

⊠ Floating Islands

This is a very old English recipe and is sometimes known as Snow Eggs. Oddly enough, today it is more popular in France than in England. *Serves 4–6.*

Custard

ISLANDS:
5 egg whites
6 tablespoons sugar
Salt
CARAMEL:
4 tablespoons sugar
2 tablespoons water

Pour the Custard into a deep dish.

Islands: Beat the egg whites until they are stiff, then fold in the sugar and a pinch of salt, using a metal spoon.

Bring a large saucepan of water to a slow boil and drop rounded tablespoons of the mixture into the boiling water. Poach for 2 minutes, gently turn them over and poach for a further 2 minutes. Lift them out very carefully with a draining spoon and cool them on paper towels.

When all of the "islands" have been poached, place them very gently on the custard and chill for 2 hours.

Caramel: Just before serving, boil the sugar and water in a small saucepan, and when it is syrupy pour it over the islands so that it makes a trail of golden threads. Serve immediately before the islands melt.

▨ Syllabub

The Italians may have Zabaglione but the British have Sylla-bub! Both are gastronomic achievements of a high order, and both make a fitting finale to a grand occasion. Syllabub is a very old recipe that dates back to Elizabethan times, when it was made with warm milk taken straight from a cow and mixed with cider and fruit juice. Serve Shortbread with your Syllabub. *Serves 6.*

Juice and grated rind of 2 lemons
½ cup sherry
3 tablespoons sugar
2 cups heavy cream
¼ teaspoon nutmeg
6 twists of lemon peel

Place the lemon juice, grated rind, sherry and sugar in a bowl. Cover and leave in a cool place for at least 1 hour.

Strain the liquid into another bowl and add the cream. Beat with a whisk or an electric beater until the cream gets thick and begins to make ribbons, then pour it into individual glasses. Chill in the refrigerator for at least 2 hours.

Before serving, sprinkle a little nutmeg and place a twist of lemon peel on top of each portion.

◪ Gooseberry Fool

Gooseberry Fool is believed to date back to the fifteenth century. It is extremely simple to prepare as its only ingredients are fruit, cream and sugar. If no gooseberries are available, rhubarb, fresh cranberries or red currants all make good substitutes as they have the same kind of sharp, tart flavor that is an absolute essential of a good fool. *Serves 4–6.*

1 pound gooseberries
1 ounce butter
3 tablespoons sugar
1½ cups heavy cream

Pinch the ends off the gooseberries. Melt the butter in a heavy saucepan and add the gooseberries and sugar. Cover the saucepan and cook over the lowest heat possible until the gooseberries are soft and mushy (approximately ½ hour).

Remove the gooseberries from the saucepan and beat them to a pulp with a wooden spoon. Pass them through a sieve and discard the skins and pips. At this point you should taste the gooseberries and if they are too tart add a little more sugar. Set them aside and allow to cool completely.

Whip the cream and fold it gently into the gooseberry pulp. Pour the fool into a glass serving dish or, if you prefer, divide it equally into small sherbet glasses. Chill for at least 1 hour before serving.

▣ Flummery

Flummery is the rather improbable sounding name of a slippery, white custard jelly. All the great ladies of English cookery —Mrs. Beeton, Mrs. Glasse and Mrs. Raffald—have their own favorite recipes. Since the dish is a very old one, there are many variations. This version uses an interesting combination of ground and chopped almonds.

If you own an old earthenware jelly mold this would be the time to use it; a copper mold would also work well. For a spectacular effect, serve the Flummery on a large white dish surrounded by lots of fresh raspberries or strawberries. *Serves 6.*

2 cups heavy cream
1 cup light cream
¼ cup chopped almonds
¼ cup ground almonds
¼ cup sugar
5 drops almond extract
2 envelopes gelatin (2 tablespoons)

Put all the ingredients except the gelatin in a saucepan and heat gently, stirring constantly, until the mixture comes to a boil. Remove from the heat and allow to cool.

Dissolve the gelatin in 2 tablespoons of boiling water and add it to the mixture. Stir well and pour the whole mixture into a jelly mold or a bowl that has been rinsed out in very hot water. Cover the mold with aluminum foil and refrigerate overnight.

Just before serving, dip the mold in hot water for a few moments and then turn the flummery onto a serving dish. Surround it with fresh fruit and serve.

◪ Port Jelly

Jellies were a popular dessert in the seventeenth and eighteenth centuries. In those days the setting agent was either a glutinous substance obtained by cooking a calf's foot or *isinglass,* which is made from the bladder of a fish. The availability of commercially produced gelatin has for some reason relegated jellies to the nursery. This is a pity, for if made with wine or real fruit juice, a jelly can be a sophisticated dessert.

This recipe is definitely intended for the grown-ups and would hardly be appreciated in the nursery. It is particularly good since half of the port is never cooked and so loses none of its rich, tawny taste. Serve with lots of whipped cream. *Serves 4.*

2½ cups port
1 envelope gelatin (1 tablespoon)
2 teaspoons lemon juice
8 tablespoons sugar
Nutmeg
Cinnamon

Place ½ cup of the port in a saucepan and soak the gelatin in it until it has completely dissolved. Stir in another cup of port together with the lemon juice and sugar. Add a pinch of nutmeg and cinnamon and bring the mixture almost to a boil over low heat, stirring constantly.

Strain into a pitcher and stir in the rest of the port. Pour the jelly into individual glasses and allow it to set for at least 2 hours.

◪ Old English Rhubarb Jelly

This is a rather unusual recipe that combines rhubarb and strawberries to make a delightfully old-fashioned jelly dessert. *Serves 6.*

2 *pounds rhubarb*
1 *cup water*
2 *envelopes gelatin (2 tablespoons)*
9 *tablespoons sugar*
1 *cup strawberries, washed and hulled*
1 *cup heavy cream*

Wash and cut the rhubarb into small chunks and put them in a saucepan with the water. Bring to a boil and simmer until the rhubarb is very soft.

Remove the saucepan from the heat and strain the rhubarb through a double thickness of cheesecloth. (Mash down the rhubarb with a wooden spoon so as to extract all the juice.)

Place half a cup of the strained juice in a bowl that has been placed in a pan of hot water. Stir in the gelatin, and when it is completely dissolved, add the rest of the juice and the sugar. Continue to stir until the sugar has dissolved. Set aside.

Puree the strawberries in a blender or food processor. Stir them into the juice and pour the mixture into a ring mold that has been dampened. Refrigerate and allow to set for at least 2 hours.

Just before serving, turn the jelly mold onto a serving dish, whip the cream and place it in the middle.

◪ Ice Cream

Commercial ice cream sold in Britain today compares poorly with its American, French and Italian counterparts. However, in Edwardian times, British ice cream was considered the best in Europe. Here are two recipes dating back to that time. Both are rich, unusual and delicious.

◪ Brown Bread Ice Cream

Serves 6.

3 cups fresh brown breadcrumbs
2 cups heavy cream
8 tablespoons confectioners' sugar
2 egg yolks
1 tablespoon rum
2 egg whites

Preheat the oven to 350°.

Spread the breadcrumbs over a large baking sheet and toast them in the oven until they become crisp and slightly browned, about 10 minutes. Remove them from the oven and set aside.

Beat the cream with the sugar until it is stiff. Mix in the egg yolks and the rum and continue to beat. In another bowl beat the egg whites, and when they are stiff fold them into the cream and sugar mixture.

As soon as the breadcrumbs are cool, fold them into the mixture and transfer it to a glass serving dish.

Freeze the ice cream for at least 4 hours before serving.

◫ Tea Ice Cream

Serves 6.

4 egg yolks
7 tablespoons sugar
2 cups heavy cream
*½ cup very strong cold China tea (3 teaspoons of tea to 1 cup
    of water)*

Beat the egg yolks in a bowl with the sugar.

Bring the cream to just below the boiling point in a saucepan over low heat. Remove from the heat and stir in the egg yolks and tea.

Cook over very low heat until the mixture begins to thicken.

Sieve the cream into a dish and freeze it for at least 4 hours before serving. (Stir it once or twice while it is freezing.)

Tea

Cucumber Sandwiches
Banana Tea Loaf
Aunt Rachel's Scones
Singin' Hinnies
Crumpets
Hot Cross Buns
Oatcakes
Eccles Cakes
Richmond Maids of Honor
Rock Cakes
Yorkshire Fat Rascals
Bosworth Jumbles
The Trumpington Ladies' Crunchy Chocolate Biscuits
Brandy Snaps
Shortbread
Mince Pies
Sticky Gingerbread
Victoria Sponge
Madeira Cake
Old-Fashioned Walnut Cake
Glazed White Icing
Sticky Topped Cake
Rosemary's Moist Chocolate Cake
Chocolate Frosting
Guinness Cake
Dundee Cake
Welsh Funeral Cake

There are few hours in life more agreeable than the
hour dedicated to the ceremony known as afternoon tea.
—Henry James, *Portrait of a Lady*

Tea must be the best known of all English gastronomic and social institutions. It can mean anything from a simple "cuppa" to an elegant spread that includes a dazzling array of sandwiches, cakes, scones and biscuits served on one's best china and centered around a steaming pot of tea.

Dutch traders first brought tea from China to England at the beginning of the seventeenth century. In those days, a pound of tea cost almost $28 and, not surprisingly, it was considered a luxury. Supplies gradually became more plentiful, and in spite of the wrath of social reformers like Jonas Hanway who declared, "Your very chambermaids have lost their bloom; I suppose by drinking tea," it quickly became the most popular drink in England. Today, the English consume 475 million pounds of tea a year, which works out to be about six cups a day for each person.

The custom of afternoon tea is credited to Anna, the seventh Duchess of Bedford, who lived in the eighteenth century. She apparently had complained of "a sinking feeling" in the afternoon and succeeded in remedying this problem with tea, cakes, friends and delicious gossip. The fashion caught on, and afternoon tea quickly became all the rage, enhanced no doubt by the strident disapproval of William Cobbett, a leading radical of his day. He believed that tea was "a debaucher of youth and a maker of misery for old age" and that "the gossip of the tea table is no bad preparatory school for the brothel."

A tea party is a cosy affair: the ideal time to entertain a few friends—not too many, as part of the regimen is to be able to talk comfortably and quietly. Not that a tea party should be all that casual an affair. Adrian Bailey in his book *The Cooking of the British Isles* recalls how an American friend of his was invited to tea in London and, becoming alarmed at the prospect of having to participate in a performance with which he was only slightly familiar, asked an English friend for guidance.

"Isn't there some kind of tea ritual?"

"Heavens, no!"

"But don't you stand in front of a low table and the lady of the house sits behind it and there's lots of silver and porcelain cups and a special cake knife and sugar tongs? And you're expected to talk about the weather and how the garden is going and doesn't she ask you whether you take milk or lemon with your tea?"

"Well of course," came the reply, "but there's no ritual!"

Certainly tea is a serious British institution, and as if to prove it there is an extraordinary repertory of regional specialties that are traditionally served for tea in different parts of the country: Shortbread and Dundee Cake from Scotland, Richmond Maids of Honor, Bath Buns, Eccles Cakes, Yorkshire Fat Rascals and all kinds of scones and biscuits. However, although the British consider tea a meal not be missed, the most famous tea party of all time, which took place in Boston on December 16, 1773, has still left something of a tempest in the American teapot. But perhaps the time has now come to reconsider its merits.

As a way of entertaining, a proper sit-down tea offers some very practical advantages. In these times of high inflation it is easy on the pocketbook. It is the perfect way to entertain friends with children; the four-to-six hour is convenient for any age, particularly on weekends, and since the essence of any good tea party is lots of variety, there is always something for everyone to eat. (I have never yet met the child who did not succumb to hot scones.)

Tea can also be organized around an activity such as bridge, tennis or a committee meeting, or one can invite friends back for tea after a football game or a day of cross-country skiing.

What other occasion gives you the opportunity to bring out Great-aunt Agatha's teapot, use that old cake plate gathering dust at the back of the closet, polish off those tarnished sugar tongs and put them back into service one last time?

To make a good cup of tea:

1. Fill the kettle with cold tap water.
2. Bring the kettle to a rapid boil.
3. Pour a little water from the kettle into a teapot, swirl it around and then pour it away. (This is known as "warming the pot.")
4. Put one generous teaspoon of tea per person plus one spoon for the pot itself in the teapot.
5. Pour the boiling water into the teapot.
6. Replace the lid on the teapot and allow the tea to brew for 5 minutes before serving.
7. Refill the kettle with more water and bring it to a boil so that you will have water on hand to replenish the teapot when necessary.
8. There is an age-old controversy as to whether the milk should be poured into the cup before or after the tea. (The former is considered very non-U.) Regardless of which way you choose to do it, be sure that the milk is cold and that it really is milk and not cream.

Different blends of tea:

ASSAM: A heavy, pungent tea from Northern India that is used in many blends.

CEYLON: Strong and dark.

DARJEELING: A delicate, amber-colored tea that is grown in the foothills of the Himalayas.

EARL GREY: A blend of Darjeeling and China tea that is scented with spices. Light and delicate and good for afternoon tea.

ENGLISH BREAKFAST: A rich blend of China and Indian tea.

LAPSANG SOUCHONG: A China tea that has a smoky flavor and comes mainly from Taiwan.

RUSSIAN: A blend of Chinese teas with a good, robust flavor.

AMERICAN BLACK: A cover-all name for all the lesser grades of tea that are used in tea bags and tend to be somewhat bland and uninteresting.

◼ Sandwiches

Sandwiches were the invention of the Earl of Sandwich. He was a compulsive gambler who evidently couldn't bear to leave the gaming table even for a meal. His solution: the sandwich. He lived in the eighteenth century, and since that time sandwiches have been an essential part of a proper English tea.

The bread for tea sandwiches must be very fresh and sliced very thin. The best way to do this is to spread the butter, which must be soft, on the bread before cutting each slice. Use a knife that has a good serrated edge for cutting the bread and remove the crusts as soon as you have cut the slice. Achieving an evenly and thinly cut slice of bread is not the easiest thing to do. Don't be discouraged; the British have had years of practice.

Sandwiches must be thin, fresh and delicate. When a waitress once brought Oscar Wilde a plate of cucumber sandwiches, which he had ordered, he turned to her and said, "My dear, I asked for a cucumber sandwich, not a loaf with a field in the middle of it."

Chicken, cucumber, watercress, ham, smoked salmon and anchovy paste all make good fillings for sandwiches. Sandwiches do not keep well and they should never be kept overnight. Try to make them as close to teatime as possible, but if you must prepare them ahead of time, wrap them in plastic and store them in a cool place.

◼ Cucumber Sandwiches

Serves 4.

1 cucumber, peeled and very thinly sliced
10 slices buttered bread, thinly sliced with crusts removed
Salt
Freshly ground pepper

Place the cucumber slices on half the slices of bread. Sprinkle with a little salt and pepper. Cover with the remaining slices and cut each slice into four triangles. Arrange on a serving plate.

⊠ Banana Tea Loaf

This tea bread contains no yeast and is simple and quick to prepare. It keeps well and even seems to improve with age, so long as it is stored in an airtight container.

2½ cups flour
2¼ teaspoons baking powder
¾ teaspoon allspice
½ teaspoon salt
8 tablespoons sugar
4 ounces butter
1 tablespoon honey
1 cup white raisins
4 medium-sized ripe bananas, mashed
2 eggs
Juice of 1 lemon

Preheat the oven to 350°.

Mix the flour, baking powder, allspice, salt and sugar in a bowl. Cut the butter into small pieces and add it and all the remaining ingredients. Mix well with an electric beater or by hand and turn the mixture into a greased 9-inch loaf pan.

Bake at 350° for 1 hour. Turn the oven down to 300° and bake for an additional ½ hour. Remove from the oven and allow the loaf to cool slightly before turning it onto a rack to cool fully.

Cut into slices and serve with butter.

⊠ Aunt Rachel's Scones

Scones are very easy to make and should be eaten right away as they do not keep well. (There is nothing in the world more dreary than day-old Scones.) Traditionally, Scones are served for tea while still warm from the oven, cut in half and spread with butter and lots of strawberry jam. They are fattening, indigestible and quite glorious. *Makes 8–10.*

2¼ cups flour
¼ teaspoon salt
½ teaspoon baking soda
1 teaspoon cream of tartar
3 ounces butter
1 heaped tablespoon honey
Approximately ¼ cup milk

Preheat the oven to 450°.

Sift the flour, salt, baking soda and cream of tartar into a mixing bowl. Rub in the butter with your fingers until the mixture resembles fine breadcrumbs. Make a well in the center and stir in the honey and enough milk to make a light springy dough, which should be just firm enough to handle.

Turn the dough onto a well-floured board. Knead very lightly to remove any cracks and roll out to a thickness of ¼ inch. Cut into 2-inch rounds with a cookie cutter or a glass. Place the rounds on a baking sheet that has been greased and floured.

Glaze each scone with a little milk and bake on the top rack of the oven for 7 to 10 minutes or until the scones have risen and are nicely browned.

⊠ Singin' Hinnies

Singin' Hinnies come from Northumberland and are traditionally cooked on a griddle; however, a heavy frying pan will do
just as well. Their curious name comes from the word "hinnie,"
which is a local corruption of the word "honey"—a common
term of endearment in the north of England. Since the hinnies
"squeak" while they cook, they have always been known as
Singin' Hinnies. *Makes approximately 18.*

2½ cups flour
2 teaspoons baking powder
¼ teaspoon salt
2 ounces butter
2 ounces lard
¾ cup currants
Approximately ¼ cup milk
Oil
Butter

Sift the flour, baking powder and salt into a bowl. Rub in the
butter and lard with your fingers until the mixture resembles
coarse breadcrumbs. Stir in the currants and add enough milk
to make a firm dough.

Roll out the dough on a well-floured surface to about ¼ inch
thickness and cut it into rounds about 2¼ inches in diameter.

Grease a heavy frying pan or a griddle with a little oil and
warm it over low heat.

Place 3 or 4 of the cakes in the pan and cook them for about
6 minutes on each side until they are well browned.

Remove them from the pan, slice them in half and place a generous knob of butter in the middle before putting them back
together. Keep them warm in the oven until all of the cakes
are cooked.

Serve immediately.

◪ Crumpets

Crumpets and muffins should be familiar to any reader of Victorian novels. Sadly, the muffin man who used to stand on the street corner ringing his bell is gone forever, and strangely enough it is in America and not in England that the so-called English muffin now thrives. However, although muffins have all but vanished in England, Crumpets (a kind of flat, yeast scone with holes on the surface), often called Pikelets, are still available in many bakeries, especially in the north of England. *Makes approximately 12–15.*

2½ cups flour
⅔ cup water
¼ ounce active dry yeast (1 envelope)
1 teaspoon sugar
Salt
2 tablespoons oil

N.B.: In order to make crumpets you will need 3 or 4 circular cookie cutters. If you don't own any, a good substitute would be to remove both ends from an empty can that is approximately 3 inches wide and 2 inches deep.

Sift the flour into a bowl and stand it on top of the stove. Heat the water in a saucepan over low heat until it is lukewarm. Take out 3 tablespoons of water and mix with the yeast and sugar in a cup.

Make a well in the flour and pour in first the yeast mixture and then the remaining water and a pinch of salt. Beat hard for 3 minutes, cover the bowl and stand it in a warm place until the dough is well risen. (This should take about 45 minutes.)

Beat the dough down and add a little warm water to turn the dough to a batter consistency.

Grease a pancake griddle or a large frying pan with a little of the oil. Place the cookie cutters on the griddle or frying pan and when the oil is hot, pour in enough dough to reach about ¾-inch high. Cook them for a few minutes until the bottoms are brown, the tops have become solid and holes have appeared all over the surface. (If the batter is too thick this will not happen and you should add more water to it.) Remove the rings, turn the crumpets and cook them for about 2 more minutes before removing them from the heat and draining on a paper towel. Repeat this process until you have used up all the dough.

Toast the crumpets and serve with lots of butter.

⊠ Hot Cross Buns

Buns are a way of life in England: Bath Buns, Chelsea Buns and probably best known of all, Hot Cross Buns, which are traditionally eaten on Good Friday. The Old Bunn House in Pimlico, London, that Swift mentions in his *Journal to Stella* (1712) used to be one of London's most famous buildings, but it is no longer standing. George II and George III, both of whom were avid bun eaters, were regular customers, and on one Good Friday in the nineteenth century almost a quarter of a million buns were reported to have been consumed on the premises. *Makes 10–12.*

½ cup milk
½ ounce active yeast (2 envelopes)
1 teaspoon sugar
2¼ cups flour
½ teaspoon salt
1 tablespoon brown sugar
¼ teaspoon nutmeg
¼ teaspoon cinnamon
¼ teaspoon cloves
¼ teaspoon ginger
1 ounce softened butter
1 egg
½ cup currants
GLAZE:
2 tablespoons milk
2 tablespoons sugar

Warm the milk gently until lukewarm and mix it with the yeast and sugar.

Place the flour in a large bowl and add the salt, brown sugar and spices. Make a well in the center and add the yeast mixture, softened butter, egg and the remaining milk so that it makes a firm dough. Add the currants. Knead the mixture until the dough takes on a rubbery texture. Cover the bowl and let it stand for 2 hours in a warm place so that the dough doubles its volume.

Punch the dough down; shape into buns and put them on 2 well-greased baking trays. Allow to rise until double their size (approximately ½ hour), then make a cross in each bun with a knife.

Bake at 400° for 15 to 20 minutes.

Just before the buns are ready to come out, boil the milk and sugar in a small saucepan until the mixture bubbles and forms a glaze.

Remove the buns from the oven and brush them while they are still hot with two coatings of glaze.

▩ Oatcakes

Oatcakes are eaten in all parts of Scotland. They are wonderfully versatile and can be served with cheese, pâté, potted meat or, best of all, still hot from the oven spread with butter and honey. *Makes approximately 12.*

2 cups plus 2 tablespoons oatmeal
½ teaspoon baking soda
Salt
1 ounce butter, melted
Approximately 6 tablespoons water

Preheat the oven to 350°.

Combine 2 cups of the oatmeal with the baking soda and a pinch of salt. Add the melted butter and the water, a tablespoon at a time, until you have a stiff but pliable dough.

Spread the remaining 2 tablespoons of oatmeal on a pastry board and roll out the dough to approximately ⅛-inch thickness. Using a wine glass, cut the dough into 3-inch rounds.

Bake the rounds on a greased baking sheet for 15 minutes, or until they begin to turn a golden brown color. Turn off the heat and leave them in the oven with the door open for 5 more minutes.

Allow to cool and store in an airtight container.

◫ Eccles Cakes

Eccles Cakes are a Lancashire specialty, named after the town of the same name. They were very popular in the seventeenth century until they were banned (along with mince pies) in 1650 by the Puritans, who thought they were sinfully rich. Oliver Cromwell went so far as to pass an act of Parliament authorizing imprisonment of any person found guilty of eating a currant pie. However, by the time of the Restoration, Eccles Cakes were being eaten again, and in 1835 the Old Original Eccles Cake Shop was opened in Eccles. It is still in business today, dispatching Eccles Cakes to all parts of the world. *Makes approximately 10.*

Puff Pastry
4 ounces currants
½ teaspoon allspice
¼ teaspoon nutmeg
3 tablespoons brown sugar
2 ounces butter
Milk
Sugar

Preheat the oven to 400°.

Prepare the pastry according to the recipe for Beef Wellington. Roll it out and cut into 4-inch rounds.

Mix the currants, allspice, nutmeg, sugar and butter in a small saucepan. As soon as the butter has completely melted remove the mixture from the heat, transfer it to a bowl and allow to cool.

Put a teaspoon of the mixture on each pastry round. Moisten the edges with a little milk, bring together and pinch to seal. Turn over and gently flatten each round with a rolling pin. Make three parallel slits across the top, brush with milk and sprinkle on a little sugar.

Place the cakes on a greased baking tray and cook them for 15 to 20 minutes or until they are nicely golden.

Remove and sprinkle the cakes with a little more sugar. Serve as soon as possible.

▨ Richmond Maids of Honor

The original recipe for these almond custard cakes is a well-kept secret handed down from generation to generation by the Newens family, who still prepare and sell Maids of Honor today. Their shop used to be in the middle of Richmond, but in 1858 they moved to Kew, which is the next-door town.

There are a number of conflicting stories as to the origin of Maids of Honor. One version is that Henry VIII used to buy them for Anne Boleyn. Another is that it was Elizabeth I who used to send her ladies-in-waiting into Richmond to purchase them for her. We will probably never know for sure with which member of royalty they first found favor, but to this day there is a terrace of houses in Richmond called Maids of Honor Row. *Makes 12–15.*

Puff Pastry
3 egg yolks
½ cup sugar
½ cup ground almonds
Grated rind and juice of 1 lemon
¼ cup heavy cream
Nutmeg

Preheat the oven to 350°.

Follow the directions for making puff pastry in the recipe for Beef Wellington. Roll out the pastry to about ¼-inch thickness and cut it into 3-inch rounds. Fit the rounds into well-greased muffin trays.

Put the egg yolks in a mixing bowl and beat in the sugar, almonds, lemon peel and juice. Add the cream and a pinch of nutmeg last and beat until the mixture is smooth.

Put a little of the mixture in each pastry shell and bake for 20 minutes or until the filling has turned golden and is almost set.

Remove the tarts from the oven and allow them to cool slightly before serving.

⊠ Rock Cakes

In spite of their name, these cakes become rocklike only if left out for several days. They are quick and simple to prepare and taste pleasant. *Makes approximately 15.*

2 cups flour
1½ teaspoons baking powder
3 tablespoons sugar
4 ounces softened butter
1 cup currants
2 beaten eggs
¼ cup milk

Preheat the oven to 350°.

Combine the flour, baking powder and sugar in a bowl. Cut the butter into small pieces and rub it in until the mixture resembles coarse breadcrumbs. Stir in the currants, eggs and milk, mixing to form a stiff batter.

Drop rounded tablespoons of the batter onto a well-greased baking sheet about 2 inches apart. Bake until they are golden in color—about 15 minutes.

Cool them on a rack.

⊠ Yorkshire Fat Rascals

This is an old recipe from Yorkshire that is a good standby for teatime. Fat Rascals are very simple currant cookies much loved by most children. *Makes approximately 12.*

2 cups flour
Generous ½ teaspoon baking powder
Salt
1 tablespoon dark brown sugar
4 ounces butter
½ cup currants
1 tablespoon milk
2–3 tablespoons water
Sugar

Preheat the oven to 400°.

Sift the flour and baking powder. Add a pinch of salt, mix in the brown sugar and rub in the butter. Add the currants, milk and just enough water to make a soft dough.

Roll out the dough on a well-floured surface to approximately ½-inch thickness and using a glass, cut into 2-inch rounds. Dust each round with a little sugar and place on a well-greased baking pan.

Bake for 20 minutes or until the Rascals begin to turn golden.

Cool on a rack before serving.

⊠ Bosworth Jumbles

Richard III sustained several losses at the battle of Bosworth in 1485. First he dropped his crown, which was picked up by the Earl of Richmond who that evening became Henry VII; then his cook mislaid the recipe for his favorite biscuits (known ever since as Bosworth Jumbles) and later in the day Richard even lost his life. *Makes 12–15.*

6 ounces butter
1¼ ounces sugar
2 eggs
2¼ cups flour

Preheat the oven to 350°.

Cream together the butter and sugar until light and fluffy. Beat in the eggs. Sift the flour and add it to the mixture.

Shape the dough into small S shapes and place them on a well-greased baking tray. Bake for 25 minutes or until they are golden brown.

◪ The Trumpington Ladies' Crunchy Chocolate Biscuits

My aunt found this recipe in a privately printed collection of recipes assembled by the ladies of Trumpington, which is a small village near Cambridge. I have slightly adapted it so as to use everyday ingredients. However, the real credit for these cookies, which are rich and sticky and do not even need baking, belongs to the Trumpington ladies. *Makes approximately 15.*

4 ounces butter
3 tablespoons sugar
6 tablespoons dark corn syrup
2 tablespoons cocoa
½ pound Honey Grahams, broken in small pieces

Melt the butter, sugar and syrup over low heat but do not allow to boil. Add the cocoa and mix well. Remove the mixture from the heat and stir in the crushed and broken Honey Grahams.

Press the mixture into a well-greased square cake pan and leave overnight in a cool place to set.

Cut the biscuits into squares or thin fingers, remove from the pan and serve.

◧ Brandy Snaps

These sticky, cylindrical snaps tasting of ginger and brandy and filled with whipped cream are delicious. They are impossible to eat without making a mess and are definitely not for picnics. *Makes approximately 15.*

2 ounces butter
4 tablespoons light corn syrup
6 tablespoons sugar
½ cup flour
1 teaspoon brandy
½ teaspoon ground ginger
1 cup heavy cream

Preheat the oven to 300°.

Heat the butter, corn syrup and sugar in the top half of a double boiler over low heat. Stir constantly until the sugar dissolves and the mixture is smooth.

Remove from the heat and stir in the flour, brandy and ginger until smooth.

Drop rounded teaspoons of the batter about 4 inches apart on a well-greased baking sheet. Bake, 4 or 5 at a time, until the snaps spread into circles and turn a golden brown. (This takes approximately 6 to 8 minutes.)

Allow the snaps to cool slightly and then loosen them from the baking sheet with a knife or spatula. Working quickly, put them one at a time in the palm of your hand and place a greased wooden handle over the center of the snap. Wrap the snap around the handle to form a cylinder. Hold in place until set, then slide the snap onto a rack. Repeat until all the snaps are finished. If the snaps become too stiff to roll, return the baking sheet briefly to the oven so that they can soften up.

Whip the cream until stiff and fill each snap with cream at both ends.

◪ Shortbread

Shortbread is traditionally eaten at Christmas time. In Scotland it is an old custom to offer Shortbread to the "first footers," those who are first to enter your house on New Year's Day.

1¾ cups flour
4 tablespoons sugar
4 ounces butter
1 egg yolk
2 tablespoons milk
Sugar

Sift the flour into a bowl. Add the sugar and rub the butter in with your fingers until the mixture is crumbly. Make a well in the center of the bowl and pour in the egg yolk and milk. Work into a smooth dough.

Transfer the dough to a cake pan 8 inches in diameter and press it out to the sides with your fingers. Crimp the edges with a fork and mark it into slices. Chill in the refrigerator for 30 minutes.

Heat the oven to 400° and bake the shortbread for 5 minutes. Turn down the heat to 300° and bake for another 30 minutes or until the shortbread begins to turn a light golden color.

Remove it from the oven and cut it into slices while it is still warm. However, do not attempt to take it out of the pan until it has fully cooled. Sprinkle with a little sugar before serving.

◪ Mince Pies

Mince Pies are traditionally served at Christmas. The earliest pies were shaped like boats and contained meat as well as spices. At the time of the Reformation, Mince Pies were considered Popish or anti-Protestant, since a mince pie was supposed to represent the cradle of the Christ child filled with the Wise Men's gifts, and for a short time they were outlawed. However, the laws were later relaxed and Mince Pies reappeared and have been a part of Christmas ever since. *Makes approximately 12 individual pies.*

8 ounces Shortcrust Pastry (use half the ingredients given for
   Shortcrust Pastry)
8 ounces Mincemeat
1 egg
Sugar

Roll out the pastry until it is about ¼-inch thick. Cut it into 3-inch rounds with a glass and place a tablespoon of Mincemeat on ½ the pastry rounds.

Beat the egg and use a little of it to moisten the edges of each round. Put a pastry top on each mincemeat patty and press the edges together with a fork.

Cut a small slit in the top of each pie, brush with the remaining egg and bake at 400° for 10 minutes. Reduce the heat to 350° and bake for a further 10 minutes or until the pies are golden. Remove the pies from the oven, dust with sugar and serve hot.

(If you wish to prepare the pies ahead of time they can be reheated for 20 minutes in a 250° oven.)

◪ Sticky Gingerbread

Good and sticky!

8 ounces butter
1 cup plus 2 tablespoons dark brown sugar
1¼ cups molasses or dark corn syrup
2 beaten eggs
2¼ cups flour
2 teaspoons ground ginger
1 tablespoon cinnamon
3 tablespoons warm milk
1 teaspoon baking soda

Preheat the oven to 300°.

Melt the butter, sugar and molasses over low heat in a medium-sized saucepan. Add the eggs, flour and spices and mix well. Add the milk and baking soda.

Remove the mixture from the heat and pour into a well-greased square 9-inch cake pan. Bake for 40 minutes and remove from the oven.

Cut the gingerbread into small square slices and allow it to cool before serving.

◫ Victoria Sponge

In the eighteenth century an English sponge cake contained many eggs but had no butter in it. It was not at all unusual to have as many as 10 eggs in one cake. However, by Queen Victoria's day butter had become an acceptable ingredient, especially when someone made the discovery that its presence helped to prevent a heavy sponge flop. The Victoria Sponge, as it was soon called, quickly became very popular.

4 ounces butter
3 eggs
1 tablespoon milk
⅔ cup sugar
1 cup flour
1 teaspoon baking powder
Salt
Confectioners' sugar
FILLING:
5 tablespoons strawberry jam
1 cup heavy cream

Preheat the oven to 375°.

Melt the butter in a saucepan over very low heat and make sure that it does not boil.

Beat the eggs with the milk (both should be at room temperature). Add the sugar and beat hard.

In a separate bowl sift the flour, baking powder and a pinch of salt and fold it gently into the egg mixture. Stir in the melted butter.

Divide the mixture between 2 well-greased 7-inch cake pans and bake side by side for 12 to 15 minutes, or until well risen and golden in color.

Remove from the oven and cool for at least 10 minutes before turning the cake onto a rack.

Whip the cream until stiff, and when the cake is completely cooled, put it together with a layer of jam and a layer of cream in the middle. Dust the top with confectioners' sugar.

◫ Madeira Cake

In the nineteenth century, any visitor who came calling was likely to be offered a glass of Madeira wine and a slice of this cake—hence its name. Madeira Cake is a plain, moist cake and is, indeed, quite excellent served with a glass of wine or sherry.

8 ounces butter
1 cup sugar
4 eggs
2 cups flour
1 teaspoon baking powder
1 teaspoon grated lemon peel
3 strips citron peel

Preheat the oven to 325°.

Grease a 9-inch loaf pan and set aside. Cream the butter and sugar. Beat the eggs in a bowl over a pan of hot water and add them to the butter and sugar. Sift the flour and baking powder in a separate bowl and fold them into the mixture. Add the lemon peel and pour the batter into the loaf pan.

Smooth the top and bake for 30 minutes. Cut the citron peel into small pieces and arrange on top of the cake. Continue to cook the cake for another 30 minutes or until a knife comes out clean.

Allow the cake to cool for a few minutes before removing it from the pan. Then leave it on a wire rack to cool fully.

▨ Old-Fashioned Walnut Cake

Years ago, Fullers Tea Rooms were a familiar sight in many English towns and Fullers cakes, which came surrounded with paper straw and packed in shiny, white boxes, were a nice reminder that bought cakes could be good. Fullers Walnut Cake with its crunchy white icing was legendary. Alas, Fullers is no more. However, this Walnut Cake recipe is similar to the famous Fullers one, even though the cake does not come in a shiny, white box.

4 ounces unsalted butter
½ cup plus 2 tablespoons sugar
2 eggs
1 cup plus 1½ tablespoons flour
1½ teaspoons baking powder
½ cup coarsely ground walnuts
6 walnut halves

Preheat the oven to 350°.

Cream the butter and sugar until fluffy. Add the eggs one at a time and beat well. Sift the flour and baking powder and mix them and the ground walnuts into the mixture.

Pour the batter into a well-greased 7-inch cake pan and bake for approximately 25 to 30 minutes. (Test with a knife to see if the cake has set.)

After removing the cake from the oven, allow it to rest for 5 minutes before turning it onto a rack. Let it cool fully before icing it with Glazed White Icing.

Decorate the top with the walnut halves.

▦ Glazed White Icing

Makes enough to ice one cake.

1 egg white
1½ cups confectioners' sugar
Pinch of salt
1 teaspoon heavy cream

Beat the egg white until stiff. Sift the sugar and add it and the salt to the egg white. Continue to beat until the icing is soft and thick and stands up in small peaks. Add the cream and beat a little more.

Spread the icing over the cake and allow it to set for at least 3 hours.

▣ Sticky Topped Cake

This upside down cake is easy to make and awfully good to eat. Served with ice cream, it also makes a quick and filling dessert.

TOPPING:

2 ounces butter
1 rounded tablespoon light corn syrup
2 tablespoons brown sugar
½ cup slivered almonds
½ cup glacé cherries, halved
½ cup white raisins

1 cup flour
1 teaspoon baking powder
2 teaspoons ground ginger
½ teaspoon salt
½ cup sugar
2 eggs
4 ounces butter

Preheat the oven to 350°.

TO MAKE THE TOPPING: Melt the butter, syrup and brown sugar in a saucepan over low heat. Add the almonds, cherries and raisins and stir well. Remove and pour into the bottom of a well-greased loaf pan or a square 9-inch pan.

Next, sift the flour, baking powder, ginger and salt into a mixing bowl. Add the sugar, eggs and butter. Beat thoroughly for 2 minutes and pour into the baking pan, making sure that all the topping is covered.

Bake for 45 to 50 minutes or until the sponge is firm to the touch of a knife. Take the cake out of the oven and turn it onto a serving plate. You will probably have to use a spoon to scrape out all the topping.

Allow to cool before serving.

⊠ Rosemary's Moist Chocolate Cake

This recipe comes from one of the great twentieth-century cooks of Chichester, who on more than one occasion has even condescended to allow an American into her kitchen.

1¾ cups flour
½ cup honey
8 tablespoons dark brown sugar
3 ounces unsweetened chocolate
4 ounces butter
½ cup plus 2 tablespoons milk
1½ teaspoons baking soda
1 beaten egg

Preheat the oven to 375°.

Grease two 7-inch cake pans and set aside.

Sift the flour into a mixing bowl. Put the honey, sugar, chocolate and butter in a saucepan and stir over low heat until the chocolate and butter are completely melted. Remove from the heat and add the milk, baking soda and egg.

Add the mixture to the flour and beat it with an electric mixer or by hand until it is smooth. Then divide it between the two cake pans and place them side by side in the oven.

Bake for 20 minutes and test with a knife into the center of the cake to make sure the batter is fully cooked.

Turn the cake onto a wire rack and allow it to cool for at least 30 minutes before covering it with Chocolate Frosting, between the two layers and on top.

◫ Chocolate Frosting

A basic recipe for Chocolate Frosting. *Makes enough to fill and ice one cake.*

1 cup plus 2 tablespoons confectioners' sugar
1 ounce unsweetened chocolate or cocoa powder
1½ ounces butter
2 tablespoons water
¼ cup sugar

Sift the confectioners' sugar into a mixing bowl and set aside.

Put the chocolate, butter, water and sugar in a saucepan. Stir over low heat until the sugar has dissolved and then bring quickly to a boil.

Remove the saucepan from the heat and pour the contents over the confectioner's sugar, stirring it well to make a smooth soft icing.

Allow the icing to cool to a lukewarm temperature before spreading.

⊠ Guinness Cake

Less familiar than cakes and ale, ale in cake is, however, an addition that results in an astonishingly moist and delicious fruit cake.

8 ounces butter
1¼ cups dark brown sugar
4 eggs, lightly beaten
2¾ cups flour
2 teaspoons allspice
8 ounces raisins
8 ounces white raisins
¼ cup candied fruit peel
4 ounces chopped walnuts
1 bottle Guinness (6½ fluid ounces)

Preheat the oven to 325°.

Cream the butter and sugar together in a mixing bowl until light. Gradually beat in the eggs. Sift the flour and allspice and gradually fold them into the butter and sugar mixture. Add the raisins, candied fruit peel and walnuts. Mix well and stir in 4 tablespoons of Guinness.

Pour the mixture into a greased 7-inch round cake pan that is at least 3 inches high. Bake in the oven for 1 hour at 325°, then reduce the heat to 300° and continue to bake for an additional 1½ hours.

Remove the cake from the oven and allow to cool. Take it out of the cake pan and turn it upside down. Prick the base of the cake in many places with a skewer and spoon in about 8 tablespoons of Guinness.

Keep the cake upside down in an airtight container for 1 week before eating. During this period, pour more Guinness over it from time to time until you have used the whole bottle.

Serve the cake right side up.

◪ Dundee Cake

Dundee is famous not just for its marmalade but also for its cake, which is rich and fruity and has always been considered the proper thing for an important or auspicious occasion. Its trademark is its covering of almonds, and its virtue is that it keeps well although it must always be stored in an airtight container.

½ cup white raisins
½ cup raisins
½ cup currants
¼ cup candied fruit peel
6 candied cherries, finely chopped
½ cup ground almonds
8 ounces butter
1 cup sugar
Grated rind of 1 orange
4 eggs
2¼ cups flour
1 teaspoon baking powder
1 tablespoon sherry
¼ cup blanched almonds, split lengthwise into halves

Preheat the oven to 300°.

Grease an 8-inch cake pan at least 3 inches high and line it with greased waxed paper.

Mix the raisins, currants, peel, cherries and ground almonds together in a bowl and set aside.

Cream the butter and sugar and add the orange rind. Beat the eggs separately and gradually add them to the mixture, beating well. Sift the flour and baking powder and fold them into the mixture. Add the sherry and all the fruit. Pour into the cake pan and arrange the almonds on the top in circles.

Bake for 2 to 2½ hours or until a knife comes out clean.

Allow the cake to cool for 10 minutes and then turn it onto a wire rack and cool fully before serving.

◪ Welsh Funeral Cake

This is a very old recipe for a rich fruit cake, traditionally offered to friends and relatives after a funeral.

1 cup plus 2 tablespoons dark brown sugar
8 ounces butter
½ cup ground almonds
3 eggs
3½ cups flour
1 cup white raisins
½ cup raisins
1 cup currants
½ cup candied fruit peel
Nutmeg
Allspice

Put the sugar and butter in a saucepan with a tablespoon of water and boil for 3 minutes.

Remove the saucepan from the heat and allow the contents to cool. Stir in the ground almonds, eggs, flour, raisins, currants, fruit peel and a pinch of nutmeg and allspice.

Pour the cake mixture into a 10-inch greased cake pan and bake at 375° for 1½ hours. Reduce the heat to 350° and cook for an additional 30 minutes.

Remove the cake from the oven and turn it onto a rack. Allow the cake to cool and store it in an airtight container.

High Tea

■

Cornish Pasties
Potted Beef
Celery with Ham in Cheese Sauce
Savory Bread and Butter Pudding
Scotch Eggs
Faggots
Toad in the Hole

"In England," said Sigi, "little boys don't have dinner."
"No dinner?"
"Supper. And sometimes only high tea."
"What is this high tea?"
"Yes, well, it's tea, you know, with cocoa and scones
and eggs if you've got hens, and bacon if you've killed
a pig, and marmalade and Bovril and kippers, and you
have it late for tea, about six."
"How terrible this must be!"
"Oh no, high tea is absolutely smashing."
—Nancy Mitford, *The Blessing*

Outside of England, the curious institution called high tea is virtually unknown and even in England it has a certain ambiguity. The reason for this confusion is that it is difficult to determine at precisely what point tea is no longer just tea but becomes high tea, although most people would agree that the addition of some kind of savory dish and a certain lateness of the tea hour are two essential requirements.

High tea, in spite of its name, is not grand, formal, or solemn and is in fact very much a "downstairs" meal, a kind of farmer's supper that has been rolled back into tea. It is also a fairly recent phenomenon—dating back only to the nineteenth century. At that time a number of social changes were taking place in England. Tea had replaced coffee as the national drink and was consumed in large quantities by all, regardless of rank or income. Afternoon tea, complete with sandwiches and cakes, had become the latest fashion among the aspiring middle and upper classes who were beginning to eat their dinner in the evening rather than at the traditional midday hour.

Downstairs, dinner remained a meal to be eaten in the middle of the day, and a modest supper consisting of a simple hot dish was served in the evening. As the custom of afternoon tea began to spread, this evening supper gradually took on some of the attributes of an afternoon tea, and with the addition of cakes and sandwiches soon became known as high tea.

A further twist: Although high tea has never really caught

on "upstairs," where it is still thought to be rather déclassé, many people who as children were confined to the nursery or the downstairs kitchen for their meals hold fond memories of this delightfully informal and unstructured meal. They remember with pleasure that there were no hard-and-fast rules about where to begin and what knife not to use.

Today, in spite of its still being considered a little unfashionable, high tea remains popular, particularly in the north of England and in rural areas. It tends to be very much a family affair that takes the place of supper and is served as soon as everyone comes home from work or school. The table is laden with a veritable panoply of dishes, and cakes, biscuits, sandwiches, eggs, leftovers and cold meat pies are quite in order. There is, of course, lots of tea to drink.

As with the recipes given for Savories, most of the high-tea dishes included here make good lunches or light supper dishes. However, every so often, why not consider serving a real high tea? It fits in very well with a weekend schedule. If you do plan a high tea, be sure to include a selection of cakes and biscuits taken from the section on Tea.

⊠ Cornish Pasties

Pastry rolled out like a plate,
Piled with turmut, tates and mate,
Doubled up and baked like fate,
That's a Cornish Pasty.

The best known of all Cornish recipes is the pasty. In the nine-teenth century, Cornish Pasties were eaten at home and taken to work by the tin miners, who kept them in their pockets and ate them for lunch. When the pasties were being made, it was the custom for each family member to place his initials on one corner of a pasty so that no one else could steal a bite.

A pasty is a turnover that is usually filled with meat but may have other fillings. When times were hard and meat was scarce, the pasties were filled with potatoes and called Tiddy Oggies (tiddy being the local name for a potato), not to be confused with Priddy Oggies, which came from the town of Priddy in nearby Somerset and were filled with pork and Ched-dar cheese. In the north of England, pasties were made in the shape of a foot and were called Lancashire Foot.

Cornish Pasties come in many different sizes and used to be sometimes as long as 12 inches. The proper way to eat a pasty is to hold it in your hand, which can, of course, sometimes be quite difficult.

The recipe given here allows one generous-sized pasty for each person. However if you wish to serve Cornish Pasties at a party, make each one smaller and they will be easier to pass around. *Serves 4.*

Shortcrust Pastry
FILLING:
12 ounces chuck steak
1 medium-sized onion, finely chopped
1 turnip or 2 small carrots, finely chopped
1 large potato, finely chopped
Salt
Freshly ground black pepper
1 egg, beaten

Preheat the oven to 400°.

Prepare the pastry.

Remove any skin or gristle from the meat and chop it into very small cubes. Mix it with the vegetables and season generously with salt and pepper.

Roll out the pastry until it is approximately ¼-inch thick. Cut it into 6-inch rounds, using a plate or a saucer to measure each circle. Lay the rounds on a flat surface and place an equal portion of the steak mixture in the middle of each round in the shape of a little sausage.

Brush the rim of each pasty with a little beaten egg and bring the sides up to meet in the middle over the top of the filling. Pinch the edges together and shape each pasty into an oval mound. Make two splits on either side of the crest so that steam can escape while the pasty is cooking.

Put the pasties on a greased baking sheet and brush the outsides with the remaining egg. Bake for 20 minutes at 400°, reduce the heat to 350° and bake for 40 minutes longer.

Remove the pasties from the oven and serve warm.

◙ Potted Beef

Potting is one of the oldest known methods of preserving food and has been widely used in Britain since medieval days. Potted Beef tastes rather like a fine pâté and is good served as an hors d'oeuvre with Oatcakes. It will keep for several weeks if stored in a cool place so long as its seal of clarified butter is not broken. *Makes approximately 2 cups.*

1 pound boneless steak
2 cups white wine
1 cup Meat Stock
3 cloves
¼ teaspoon mace
1 teaspoon Worcestershire sauce
Salt
Freshly ground black pepper
2 tablespoons brandy
6 ounces butter

Cut the beef into 1-inch cubes and put them in a shallow oven-proof dish. Cover with the wine, stock, cloves, mace, Worcestershire sauce and a little salt and pepper. Cover with a lid or piece of aluminum foil and cook for 2 hours at 250°.

Remove the meat and grind to a paste in a food processor or blender. Discard the cloves and boil the juice until it is reduced to 3 tablespoons. Add this, the brandy and 2 ounces of the butter to the meat and put the mixture in 2 small pots.

Melt the remaining butter in a heavy saucepan over low heat. When it has fully melted, skim the foam off the top and spoon out the clear butter, leaving any residue on the bottom.

Pour the clear (clarified) butter over the meat and chill for several hours before serving.

⊠ Celery with Ham in Cheese Sauce

In spite of its rather prosaic name, this particular recipe is very good and makes a nice light supper or lunch dish, or could even be used as a first course for a dinner party. The combination of celery and cheese works well, although if you prefer, endive can be substituted for the celery. (*Note:* In England what Americans call endive is known as chicory and chicory is known as endive. Here I follow the American practice.) *Serves 6.*

3 celery hearts
3 cups Basic White Sauce
1 cup grated Cheddar cheese
6 slices ham
½ teaspoon nutmeg
½ cup toasted breadcrumbs
1 ounce butter

Clean and trim the celery hearts and cook them in a large pan of salted boiling water for about 15 minutes or until they are tender but not falling apart.

Meanwhile prepare the Basic White Sauce and add the cheese to it.

Cut each celery heart in half and wrap each half in a slice of ham. Sprinkle with nutmeg, lay them in a row in a shallow oval ovenproof dish and cover completely with the cheese sauce. Sprinkle the breadcrumbs over the top and dot with butter.

Bake at 400° for 20 minutes and serve hot and bubbling.

⊠ Savory Bread and Butter Pudding

If inflation has really hit or there is almost no food in the house, this dish comes in very handy. It is fine for lunch or a light supper. Serve it with a green salad. *Serves 4–6.*

6 slices buttered bread, crusts removed
1½ cups coarsely grated Cheddar cheese
Salt
Freshly ground black pepper
3 beaten eggs
2¼ cups milk
3–4 slices bacon or ham

Fill a well-greased pie or soufflé dish with layers of bread and butter. Sprinkle a total of 1 cup of cheese and a little salt and pepper over each layer and set the dish aside.

Put the eggs in a saucepan and gradually add the milk while cooking over low heat. Stir constantly and bring to just below the boiling point. Remove from heat and pour over the bread. Place the bacon or ham slices on top and cover with the remaining cheese.

Allow to stand for 15 minutes, then put the dish on the top shelf of the oven at 350°. Cook for ¾ hour or until the pudding has firmly set.

◨ Scotch Eggs

Often served in pubs, Scotch Eggs make marvelous snacks. The only way to eat them is with your fingers. For this reason, they are very useful for picnics. *Serves 6–8.*

8 small hard-boiled eggs, shells removed
Flour
2 pounds sausage meat
1½ cups fresh breadcrumbs
1 tablespoon mace
½ teaspoon salt
½ teaspoon freshly ground black pepper
2 beaten eggs
Oil for deep frying

Dust the hard-boiled eggs lightly with a little flour and set them aside.

Roll out the sausage meat on a flat surface with a pastry roller. Mix the breadcrumbs with the mace, salt and pepper and put them in a shallow dish.

Take each hard-boiled egg and dip it into the beaten egg, then put it on the sausage meat and, using your fingers, wrap the meat over the egg until it is entirely covered. Be generous with the meat—it should be at least ½-inch thick around the egg.

Once the egg is covered, roll it in the breadcrumb mixture and smooth it back into shape so that it still resembles an egg. When all the eggs have been wrapped this way, heat the oil and deep fry the eggs until they are golden brown.

Allow the eggs to cool at room temperature for at least 2 hours before serving.

◪ Faggots

Faggots is a very old dish and used to be a popular way to use up the odd bits and pieces left over from a pig. Some butchers still prepare their own faggots, but this is becoming increasingly rare. To be properly authentic, Faggots, also known as Poor Man's Goose or Savory Duck, should be cooked in the caul (the fatty veil that covers the pig's abdominal organs) and made in the shape of sausages. However, this recipe does without the caul and is a lot simpler to prepare.

4 ounces liver
8 slices bacon
6 medium-sized onions
1¼ cups water
3 cups breadcrumbs soaked in 1 cup water
½ teaspoon sage
Salt
Freshly ground black pepper

Preheat the oven to 250°.

Chop the liver, bacon and onions into small pieces. Cook the bacon and onions together in a pan over low heat for 5 minutes. Add the liver and water. Simmer the mixture for 15 minutes.

Add the soaked breadcrumbs and the sage. Season with a little salt and pepper and mix thoroughly. Turn into a well-greased square baking pan. Cut into squares and bake for 45 minutes.

Serve cold.

⊠ Toad in the Hole

This is a variation of Yorkshire Pudding and makes an excellent light supper or lunch dish. Serve it with an endive and watercress salad. *Serves 4.*

Yorkshire Pudding batter
1 pound small breakfast sausages

Preheat the oven to 450°.

Fry the sausages in a frying pan until they are crisp and well browned. Drain most of the fat but keep enough to cover the bottom of a good-sized, preheated ovenproof dish.

Make sure the fat is very hot before you put the sausages in the dish and pour on the batter.

Bake for 10 minutes at 450°. Reduce the heat to 350° and cook for another 15 minutes to make sure the batter is well risen and has turned a golden brown. (Try not to open the oven door while the toad is cooking.)

N.B.: One of my aunts used to substitute bacon for sausages. I have never seen this done anywhere else; however, it makes a nice variation.

Preserves
and
Pickles

■

Marmalade
Lemon Curd
Red Currant Jelly
Mincemeat
Red Tomato Chutney
Green Tomato Chutney
Mango Chutney
Hot Orange Chutney
Pickled Onions
Pickled Eggs
Pickled Mushrooms

The preservation of food has always required attention and ingenuity. Its very necessity in times predating refrigeration opened a whole area of taste. Pickled and spiced foods have come to play as important a role on the British table and in the British larder as in any of the world's great cuisines. Even today in many parts of Britain the larder is considered more essential than the refrigerator, and these older methods of food preservation are very much in evidence.

Village fairs and garden fêtes frequently boast an incredible array of preserved foods and the competition among jam makers is always fierce. British housewives take a great pride in their preserves and in having their pickles pronounced excellent.

Over a hundred years ago, Mrs. Beeton felt that "nothing shows more, perhaps, the difference between a tidy, thrifty housewife and a lady to whom these desirable epithets may not honestly be applied, than the appearance of their respective store closets." A well-stocked larder is still one of the first clues a visitor to a British home can have to indicate whether or not cooking is taken seriously.

DO'S AND DON'TS FOR MAKING PRESERVES
AND PICKLES

1. Don't use copper, brass or iron saucepans for cooking the fruit.
2. Use standard canning jars or jelly glasses with matching lids.
3. Wash the jars or glasses, lids and rings in hot water. Put them in a large saucepan and cover with hot water. Bring the water to a boil, remove the saucepan from the heat and let the jars or glasses stand in it until you are ready to use them. They should still be warm when you fill them.
4. Fill the jars or glasses to the top. Immediately seal them tightly with their rings and lids. Jelly glasses should be sealed with a layer of hot paraffin, which should be melted beforehand in a double boiler. Make sure that the paraffin completely covers the surface of the glass.

5. If there is not enough fruit to fill the last jar or glass completely, do not seal but refrigerate and eat the contents as soon as possible.
6. Store pickles and preserves in a dry, cool place.
7. Label and date all your pickles and preserves before you store them.

⊠ Marmalade

Marmalade originated in Scotland in the late eighteenth century. The story goes that James Keiller bought a considerable quantity of oranges off a ship that had come to Dundee from Spain. The oranges were cheap, the reason being, as he soon discovered, that they were very bitter. Unable to sell them, he took them home to his wife, who like him believed in thrift. She experimented in her kitchen and came up with what we know as marmalade. (Keillers Marmalade is still sold today.) Although Marmalade quickly became very popular in Scotland, it was not until many years later when Mrs. Frank Cooper, the wife of an Oxford grocer, began making it for undergraduates that it caught on in England. Marmalade should be made from Seville oranges. However, since they are not often available in the United States, the addition of one lemon for every three oranges makes an acceptable substitute. *Makes approximately 12 large jars.*

9 Seville oranges or 9 juice oranges and 3 lemons
21 cups water
6 pounds sugar

Wash the oranges and the lemons and put them in a large saucepan. Cover with water and boil for 2 hours.

Pour the water into a pitcher and cut the fruit into quarters, taking out the flesh and removing any pith and seeds. Cut the skin into small pieces and return it with the flesh to the saucepan. Add the water, using the water in which the fruit was previously cooked plus enough to make the 21 cups.

Bring the water and the fruit to a boil, lower the heat and add the sugar. Allow the sugar to dissolve over low heat, then bring the marmalade back to a fast boil and cook for about 30 minutes or until set. (To test for setting, pour a small amount of marmalade onto a cold saucer or an ice tray turned upside down. If it coagulates and begins to wrinkle, it is set.)

Allow the marmalade to cool for 10 minutes before pouring it into clean hot jars and sealing.

▣ Lemon Curd

Lemon Curd is easy to prepare and delicious spread on a slice of buttered bread. It has always been popular for teatime and makes a nice change from jam. While it can also be used as a filling for an open tart, I have found that a small amount of hot Lemon Curd poured over vanilla ice cream, while hardly traditional, is quite irresistible.

Once you have made a batch of lemon curd, don't put off eating it for too long; it will keep perfectly well in the refrigerator for up to 3 weeks, but should not be kept for much longer than that. *Makes approximately 3 cups.*

3 large lemons
4 ounces butter
1½ cups sugar
3 egg yolks, beaten

Wash the lemons and grate their rinds.

Squeeze and strain the lemon juice into the top of a double boiler. Add the grated peel and the butter, sugar and beaten egg yolks.

Cook gently, stirring constantly, until the sugar dissolves, the butter melts and the mixture begins to thicken. (This will take about 5 minutes.) Be careful not to let it boil or the eggs will curdle.

As soon as the lemon curd has become thick and creamy, remove it from the heat and pour it into a bowl or clean jars. Cover immediately, otherwise it will form a skin, and refrigerate as soon as it has cooled slightly.

◪ Red Currant Jelly

If you are lucky enough to be able to find red currants in the stores or if you grow your own, there is nothing that is quite so delicious as homemade Red Currant Jelly. It is traditional to serve it with lamb. *Makes approximately 9 cups.*

4 pounds red currants
3 cloves
Sugar

Put the red currants and cloves in a large saucepan. Cover with water and simmer until the fruit is soft and mushy.

Most serious jam makers in Britain have their own flannel jelly bags for jam-straining. However, if you do not possess such an object, you can improvise one by taking a large piece of muslin cheesecloth and tying each corner to the rungs of a chair that has been turned upside down and is balanced on another chair. Place a bowl underneath the cheesecloth and empty the currants onto the cheesecloth so that they strain very slowly into the bowl. It is important not to squeeze or hurry the fruit, and since this operation will take several hours, the simplest thing to do is to let it happen overnight.

Next day, for every 2½ cups of strained fruit juice measure 2¼ cups of sugar. Place the fruit and sugar in a saucepan and stir over low heat until the sugar is dissolved. Then bring the mixture to a boil and boil briskly for about 10 minutes or until the jelly has set. (To test for setting, drop a tiny bit of the jelly onto a cold saucer or an ice tray turned upside down. Allow it to cool, and if the jelly wrinkles it is set.)

Pour the jelly into clean hot jars and seal.

▨ Mincemeat

It is really worth the effort to prepare your own Mincemeat, as it will taste quite different from and far superior to anything you can buy in a store, even though it no longer contains meat as it did in the sixteenth and seventeenth centuries. Always prepare it at least 3 weeks before you plan to use it, as it really improves with age and lasts almost indefinitely. A friend of mine always makes her supply at least a year in advance. *Makes approximately 9 cups.*

1 cup shredded suet
1 cup white raisins
1 cup raisins
3 medium-sized green apples, peeled, cored and chopped
½ cup marmalade
¾ cup chopped almonds
1 cup brown sugar
½ cup mixed candied peel
1 cup currants
1 wineglass brandy
Juice of ½ a lemon
¼ teaspoon grated nutmeg
½ teaspoon ground ginger

Mix together the suet, raisins, apples, marmalade, almonds, sugar, candied peel and currants. Add the brandy, lemon juice and spices. Cover the mixture with a cloth and leave it in a cool place overnight.

Next day, mix the mincemeat thoroughly and pack and seal in glass jars.

◙ Chutney

The word "chutney" comes from the Hindustani word *chatni*, which means a hot, spicy condiment. It is a strong relish, usually served with cold meat or curry. It is also delicious served with bread and cheese and can frequently be found on the lunch menu of British pubs, accompanied, naturally, by a pint of beer.

Chutney became an accepted part of the British culinary scene after it was brought back by the British who had lived in India. Green Tomato Chutney is probably the most common. However, there are many other varieties, and since green tomatoes are sometimes hard to find unless you grow your own, I have also included some other recipes that use red tomatoes, mangoes and oranges.

◙ Red Tomato Chutney

This is a fairly mild chutney with a nice mellow flavor. *Makes approximately 9 cups.*

4 pounds red tomatoes
1 ounce mustard seeds
2 teaspoons allspice
2 teaspoons cayenne pepper
1¼ cups sugar
1 ounce salt
1¾ cups plus 2 tablespoons malt vinegar

Immerse the tomatoes in boiling water for about 1 minute, then peel.

Tie the mustard seeds and the allspice in a piece of cheesecloth and put it in a large saucepan with the tomatoes and cayenne pepper.

Bring the mixture to a boil and simmer until the tomatoes are reduced to a pulp—about 45 minutes. Add the sugar, salt and vinegar and continue to simmer for another 40 minutes.

Remove the cheesecloth, pour into hot jars and seal.

▣ Green Tomato Chutney

Makes approximately 14 cups.

6 pounds green tomatoes
6 green apples, peeled and cored
4 medium-sized onions
5–7 cups tarragon vinegar
2½ cups dark brown sugar
¼ ounce red chilies
1 teaspoon ground cinnamon
½ teaspoon whole mustard seeds
½ teaspoon cloves
½ teaspoon peppercorns
3 cups white raisins
Juice of 2 lemons
2 tablespoons salt

Mince or finely chop the tomatoes, apples and onions. Set aside. Place 5 cups of the vinegar and the sugar in a large saucepan and bring to a boil. Simmer gently until a syrup forms.

Tie the chilies, cinnamon, mustard seeds, cloves and peppercorns in a bag made out of two thicknesses of cheesecloth and put it in the saucepan, together with the tomatoes, apples and onions. Add the raisins, lemon juice and salt. Cover and simmer for 4 hours. If the chutney gets too thick, add another 1 or 2 cups of vinegar.

After 4 hours, remove the saucepan from the heat and allow it to cool slightly. Take out the bag of spices, pour the chutney into warmed jars and seal.

◪ Mango Chutney

Mango Chutney is particularly good, and since mangoes are readily available, it is well worth making. In Britain, mangoes have always been extremely scarce, and many Victorian cookery books offer their readers a number of recipes for fake mango chutney. *Makes approximately 12 cups.*

8 large green mangoes
2 tablespoons salt
2½ cups malt vinegar
1¼ cups sugar
1 teaspoon ground ginger
2 sticks cinnamon
2 tablespoons mustard seeds
2 teaspoons cayenne pepper

Peel the mangoes and slice into chunks. Put them in a bowl and sprinkle with the salt. Let stand for 24 hours in a cool place and then rinse thoroughly.

Take 1 cup of the vinegar and heat it in a large saucepan with the sugar until it forms a thick syrup. Add the rest of the vinegar and the mangoes. Tie the remaining ingredients in a piece of cheesecloth and add them.

Simmer the chutney for approximately 40 minutes or until the mixture becomes thick and syrupy. Remove the cheesecloth bag, pour the chutney into hot jars and seal.

◫ Hot Orange Chutney

Makes approximately 11 cups.

7 large oranges
1 lemon
5 large green apples, peeled and chopped
3 large onions, chopped
¾ cup white raisins
1¼ cups dark brown sugar
1 cup white sugar
1 teaspoon freshly ground black pepper
2 teaspoons ground ginger
1 teaspoon cayenne pepper
3½ cups malt vinegar

Grate the rinds of the oranges and the lemon into a large saucepan, but be sure not to grate any pith. Peel the fruit and cut the flesh into small pieces. Remove any seeds and put the fruit, apples, onions, raisins, sugar, spices and vinegar in the saucepan.

Simmer for 1 hour or until the chutney has thickened.

Pour it into clean jars and seal.

◪ Pickled Onions

Pickled Onions served with bread and cheese are part of a "ploughman's lunch." *Makes approximately 5 cups.*

14 small white onions
½ cup salt
3 cups malt vinegar
8 tablespoons sugar
10 cloves
10 peppercorns

Plunge the onions in boiling water for a few minutes to soften their skins. Drain and peel, rub with the salt and let stand overnight in a bowl.

Rinse the onions with water and dry them with paper towels.

Mix the vinegar, sugar and spices in a large saucepan and add the onions. If they are not completely covered, add a little water.

Bring gently to a boil, cover and simmer for 10 minutes or until the onions are half cooked. They should be soft on the outside but still hard in the center.

Pack them into clean, hot jars and pour the vinegar mixture over them.

Seal the jars and store them for at least 2 weeks before eating.

◪ Pickled Eggs

Pickled Eggs are a West Country specialty frequently served in pubs. They are a good standby to have on hand for lunch and are excellent with cold meat or cheese. One of their great advantages is that they keep almost indefinitely and actually seem to improve with age.

12 eggs
4 cups malt vinegar
3 cinnamon sticks
10 whole cloves
2 teaspoons allspice
10 peppercorns
1 chili pepper, finely chopped

Put the eggs in cold water, add a teaspoon of vinegar and bring them gently to a boil. Continue to boil for 10 minutes and then put them in a bowl of cold water. When they are cool enough to handle, peel off the shells and put them in clean jars (the larger the better).

Heat the vinegar and spices in the top of a double boiler. Remove from the heat as soon as the mixture comes to a boil. Allow the mixture to steep for two hours and then pour it over the eggs and seal the jars. Store at least 2 weeks before eating.

◪ Pickled Mushrooms

Makes approximately 4 cups.

5 cups small button mushrooms, washed and trimmed
1 teaspoon salt
1½ cups malt vinegar

Place the mushrooms in a pan and sprinkle with the salt. Sauté over low heat for a few minutes. Add the vinegar and simmer gently for 10 minutes.

Pack into clean jars and seal.

Cheese

Many people are astonished to learn that there is more to English cheese than Cheddar. This is hardly surprising, since English cheeses are yet another of those well-kept culinary secrets. In actual fact, there is a wide variety of English cheeses, some of which are still being made by local farmers according to traditional methods. In recent years, a renewed interest in regional cheeses has resulted in the greater availability of such cheeses as Cheshire, Leicester, Derby and Wensleydale, in addition to the better-known Caerphilly, Double Gloucester, Lancashire, Stilton and, of course, Cheddar, all of which can be obtained at most good cheese stores in the United States.

In addition to the use of cheese in many recipes (English cheeses, being mostly hard and crumbly, are particularly well suited for cooking), it is customary to offer a cheese course at an English dinner. This is correctly served after rather than before the dessert—something most foreigners find extremely confusing.

CAERPHILLY: A mild, soft, crumbly white cheese that originally came from the village of Caerphilly in Wales but is now mainly produced in the West Country. It is delicious for eating but is not recommended for cooking.

CHEDDAR: The best known and most popular of all English cheeses, Cheddar is a mature cheese that takes over a year to make. It comes in large wheels, called truckles, and the average weight of a truckle is 65 pounds. At one time Cheddar used to be eaten only by the rich, but this is no longer the case. The color of Cheddar runs from pale yellow to golden orange and it has a sweet, nutty flavor. It is wonderful for cooking and forms the mainstay of a "ploughman's lunch"—that unbeatable combination of crusty bread, a hunk of cheese, pickled onions and a pint of beer.

DERBY: A good, plain cheese with a buttery texture. A variation, Sage Derby, is made by pressing fresh sage leaves between the layers of the curd before it is pressed. This gives the cheese a green, marbled effect.

CHESHIRE: Believed to be the oldest of all English cheeses, Cheshire is mentioned in the Domesday Book and comes colored, white and blue. It is a crumbly cheese that has a nutty and slightly salty flavor and is excellent for cooking.

DOUBLE GLOUCESTER: This is a strong, dark-colored cheese with a very sharp flavor. It tends to be a little dry and is very good for making Welsh Rarebit. Not surprisingly, it comes from Gloucester and at one time on May Day a huge wheel of the cheese used to be garlanded and led around the town.

DUNLOP: A mild, soft and creamy cheese that comes from Scotland.

LANCASHIRE: A semihard, crumbly white cheese that is rather moist and has a slightly acid taste. It does not travel well.

LEICESTER: This cheese, which is mild and has a very mellow, orange-red color, is particularly good for cooking and toasting.

STILTON: "The king of English cheese," Stilton was originally known as Lady Beaumont's cheese and was made by her housekeeper in the eighteenth century. One of Lady Beaumont's daughters married a farmer from Melton Mowbray. She also made the cheese and supplied her sister, whose husband kept an inn at Stilton in Huntingdonshire, with some of it. This, of course, is how it came to be known as Stilton. Stilton used to take 18 months to mature. However, this has now been reduced to about 6 months. Stilton is patented to guard it against imitations. You will sometimes see Stilton served with a scoop, but this is incorrect as it dries out the cheese. The correct way to cut into a Stilton is to make a horizontal slice across the cheese.

WENSLEYDALE: This cheese is believed to have been brought to England by the Normans and was later made by the monks of Jervaulx in the dales of Yorkshire. It is a delicate white cheese that unfortunately is very hard to find.

Anyone seriously interested in tasting English cheese should visit Wells Stores in Streatley-on-Thames, Nr. Reading. It is unique, and the proprietor, Major Patrick Rance, is an authority on and passionate advocate of English cheeses. He has spent the last 15 years tracking down farmers in remote and faraway places who still make their own unpasteurized cheeses and follow traditional cheese-making methods.

Mr. Rance's shop offers superb examples of all the cheeses mentioned above, and he is likely also to have other much rarer cheeses on hand, such as Blue Vinny, Cotherstone and Blue Shropshire. His shop is a paradise for any serious cheese eater. If you cannot get to Streatley, Mr. Rance will ship his cheese on request to any part of the world. For further information, write to, Wells Stores, Streatley-on-Thames, Nr. Reading, Berkshire, England.

Beer

Beer is undoubtedly the national drink of England (the Scots prefer their whiskey). In Elizabethan times, it was drunk in great quantities by all social classes. When traveling, Queen Elizabeth I was always accompanied by her personal beer-taster and, as part of their remuneration, each of her ladies-in-waiting was entitled to two gallons of beer a day.

Today, most beer is consumed in pubs, and the pub remains an enduring part of the national landscape. It is also a social institution dating back to the first century A.D., when, according to a contemporary Greek visitor, "Britons were accustomed to gathering in their alehouses to govern and adjudicate." Even the smallest English village will have its pub, which is usually the center of village life—warm, welcoming, a place to meet and talk—a public house in all respects.

Pub drinking has many rituals. Serious drinkers take their beer in imperial pints (larger than an American pint) and if you are drinking with a group of friends it is customary for each member of the party to pay for a "round" of beer in strict rotation. There is a strange discrepancy between the opening and closing times of pubs in different parts of the country. This dates back to the time of World War I when the British Prime Minister, Lloyd George, who was a temperate Welshman, first introduced laws to restrict drinking hours. It seems he was worried about drunkenness, especially among munitions workers: "We are fighting Germany, Austria and drink, and the greatest of these deadly foes is drink." Since the regulations were later enforced locally, there is still little uniformity and much confusion on the matter of hours.

English beer, which should be drunk at room temperature, is something of an acquired taste. On one occasion, Lady Churchill remarked to her husband that she hated the taste of beer. To which he replied, "So do many people—to begin with. It is, however, a prejudice that many have been able to overcome."

English beer, or ale as it is often called, is brewed from malted barley, hops, yeast and water and continues to mature and ferment in the barrel even after it leaves the brewery. For this to happen, the barrel needs to be open to the air so that the carbon dioxide produced by fermentation can escape. All of this requires quite a bit of skill and care on the part of the publican, and in the 1960s, in an attempt to do away with such problems and standardize the process, the large breweries began to market national brands of beer that were stored in highly pressurized containers, artificially carbonated and fermented under pressure. This resulted in very bland beer, and during the 1970s a small group of unhappy beer drinkers came together and launched the Campaign for Real Ale (CAMRA) to generate an interest in "real ale" and force the brewers to get rid of their new-fangled brewing techniques.

The CAMRA campaign has proved incredibly successful, and more and more pubs, which previously served only artificially fermented national brands of beer, now proudly display the CAMRA sign and offer their customers beer that is brewed and served according to traditional methods. (No small victory in these days of standardization and mass production!)

"Bitter" is the name for the most common kind of everyday brew, and most bitters taste as their name suggests they should. In addition to serving their customers Bitter, most pubs will also offer a *Special* or *Best Bitter*, which tends to be more full-bodied and slightly sweeter than an ordinary Bitter. If the Bitter is not on tap and comes in a bottle, it is often referred to as *Pale Ale*, not to be confused with *Mild Ale*, a distinctive draught beer that is popular in the Midlands and Northwest of England and is fuller in flavor than ordinary Bitter. Bottled Mild Ale is usually called *Brown Ale*. *Stout* is a heavy beer made with less malt and more barley. It is dark, rich and velvety and slightly on the sweet side. *Extra Stout* is the most bitter and full-bodied of all the dark beers and has become synonymous with the name *Guinness.*

Beer goes well with English food, particularly stews and meat pies. A wide selection of English beers is now imported into the United States, and at a few American bars it is even possible to drink draught English beer (served straight from the barrel), although it is more usual for it to be bottled. Beers currently imported include Guinness, John Courage, Murphy's Irish Stout, Newcastle Brown Ale, Whitbread's Ale, Vaux, Bass and Watney's Stinge.

Ingredients

ALMONDS: Blanched, slivered and chopped almonds are available at most food stores. However, to make ground almonds, place the almonds, which should be coarsely chopped, in a blender or food processor and pulverize them for about 30 seconds. Ground almonds can also be made using a pestle and mortar. To toast almonds, spread them in a pan and place them in a 350° oven for about 10 minutes, turning frequently so they do not burn. (Four ounces of almonds equals about ¾ cup.)

APPLES: There are more than twenty-one varieties of apples in England. Unfortunately there is less choice in the United States, and in many vegetable markets the selection is limited to "red" or "green." When preparing a recipe that uses apples, try to find cooking apples. If none are available, use green apples rather than red ones.

ANCHOVY PASTE: It comes in a tube and can be purchased at most specialty food stores. You can also make your own using a can of anchovy fillets. First wash them in cold water, then mash them with a fork and add just enough olive oil to make a smooth paste.

BACON: American bacon is very different from English bacon—much streakier and, unfortunately, not nearly so good. Whenever possible use Canadian bacon, which is quite similar to English bacon.

BREADCRUMBS: Commercially prepared breadcrumbs taste so unpleasant that you should always make your own. Unless a recipe specifies "fresh" breadcrumbs, in which case use fresh bread, grate or crumble slightly stale bread in a blender or food processor. Breadcrumbs will keep for about 2 days if they are stored in a tightly closed container and are refrigerated, but not very much longer. (Four ounces of dry breadcrumbs equals about 1 cup, 4 ounces of fresh breadcrumbs equals about 2 cups.)

BROWN SUGAR: Always use soft brown sugar and never "brown-ulated."

BUTTER: Use salted butter, unless unsalted is specified in the list of ingredients.

CHEDDAR: When a recipe calls for Cheddar, use English Cheddar if possible. It really is the best and is available at most cheese stores. If you cannot obtain it, I would recommend using Vermont Cheddar as I think it is the closest in taste.

CITRON: Not to be confused with a lemon, a citron is larger, less acid and has a thicker peel. The fruit itself is not eaten but the thick rind is used as a preserve and for decoration. Citron can be found in most specialty food stores.

ENGLISH MUSTARD: English mustard comes in the form of a powder. It is much stronger than French or American mustard and is prepared by mixing the mustard powder with water according to the directions given on the package. Once English mustard has been prepared, it does not keep well, so make it in small quantities.

FLOUR: Use unbleached flour.

GOOSEBERRIES: This berry fruit has a bright green skin covered with tiny hairs. It has a very sharp flavor and should be eaten cooked and not raw.

HERBS: Whenever possible use fresh rather than dried herbs. Store fresh herbs in a tightly wrapped plastic bag in the refrigerator.

KIPPERS: Kippers are herrings that have been split down the middle and cold-smoked in a solution of brine. It is almost impossible to find Scotch kippers in this country. However, Canadian kippers, which are extremely good, can be found in many stores that offer smoked fish. Failing this, you can always obtain canned kipper fillets.

LARD: Lard is the rendered-down fat from a pig. It has a greater shortening effect than butter and gives shortcrust pastry an added crispness. Available at any supermarket.

MADEIRA: A deep amber-tinted wine that is made from white grapes and comes from the island of Madeira. It resembles a well-matured, full-bodied sherry.

OIL: For cooking, use vegetable or peanut oil. Olive oil is too strong and should be kept for salads.

PEPPER: Keep a supply of peppercorns handy and always grind your own pepper.

PORT: A strong, dark red wine that comes from Portugal and was traditionally drunk by gentlemen at the end of dinner when they withdrew from the ladies to smoke their cigars.

RED CURRANT: The red currant is a bright red fruit that is very juicy and should be cooked before eating. It is mostly used for jams and jellies.

RHUBARB: Rhubarb has long red stalks that are white at the base and sprout into green leaves at the top. It has an extremely tart flavor and should not be eaten raw. The stem, not the green leaves, is used for cooking.

RICE: Don't use pre- or parcooked rice. Short-grain Carolina rice is best for puddings and soup, long-grain rice for savory dishes.

SHERRY: For cooking, use a medium-dry California sherry.

SMOKED HADDOCK: Also sometimes known as Finnan Haddock, this is a haddock that has been cold-smoked in a solution of brine. It is a bright yellow color and is used in many British dishes.

SUET: Suet is the white fatty casing that surrounds the kidneys. All butchers have suet for sale—usually beef or veal but sometimes mutton—and most of them will assume that you want it for feeding the birds! Suet is used in any pastry or pudding that needs to be steamed. It has a higher melting point than butter and when it does melt it leaves small holes in the dough, giving it a loose soft texture. To shred suet, peel off the paperlike skin and grate the remaining lumps of suet as you would grate cheese, in either a grater or food processor. If you store shredded or unshredded suet in a tightly closed jar and keep it refrigerated, it will keep for as long as three months. (Three and a half ounces of suet equals about 1 cup of shredded suet.)

Utensils

It really isn't necessary to have a huge amount of kitchen equipment, but it is important to give some thought to what you do need and what you buy. Equipment should be simple, versatile and of top quality so that it will last for a long time. Cooking utensils are not something you want to change every few years. Pots and pans should grow old with you, and those that are most indispensable are often the ones that are passed on from one generation to the next.

KNIVES: A few good knives are essential in any kitchen. Preferably they should be made of carbon steel, although a good quality stainless steel will do. The blades should extend through the wooden handle and should be held in place with rivets. Always chop food on a wooden surface and treat your knives with great care. Wash and dry them by hand after use. Don't leave them soaking in water and do not put them in the dishwasher.

SAUCEPANS: Whether you choose copper, enameled iron, aluminum or stainless steel, be sure you select thick, heavy-bottomed pans. (I would not recommend stainless steel as it does not conduct heat well.) You will need at least 3 saucepans in different sizes. All of them should have tight-fitting lids.

FRYING PANS: Choose heavy frying pans, made of either enameled iron with black interiors or steel. You will need at least 1 small and 1 large frying pan. When washing a frying pan, don't immerse it in water, simply rub it clean with a damp paper towel and then rub it with a little oil.

The following is a list of some of the other essentials that even the smallest kitchen should have.

Measuring cup
Measuring spoons
1 rolling pin
1 pastry brush
3 wooden spoons

1 spatula
An orange/lemon squeezer
1 pepper mill
1 kettle
1 colander or large sieve
1 wire whisk
1 garlic press
1 standard-size loaf pan
2 cake pans
1 cake rack
1 baking tray
1 double boiler
1 cheese grater
2 pie dishes
1 wooden chopping board
Pestle and mortar or a food processor or blender
Food mill
2 mixing bowls
2 earthenware pudding basins
Cheesecloth

N.B.: Earthenware basins known as English pudding basins or bowls are available at most kitchen equipment stores. They come in various sizes and are used for preparing steamed puddings. Usually their sizes are given in British measurements: 1¼ pint, 1¾ pint and 2½ pint are the standard sizes, but remember that the imperial pint is slightly larger than the American pint. All the recipes in this book can be prepared in basins that hold either approximately 3 cups, 5 cups or 7 cups. A Pyrex bowl can always be substituted for an English pudding bowl.

You might also want to use a china or copper mold for making such desserts as flummeries and jellies. These can be found in most kitchen equipment stores. It is also possible to find old Victorian pudding molds in many antique shops and flea markets.

Menus

A COUNTRY BREAKFAST

Porridge
Kedgeree
Deviled Kidneys
Toast and Marmalade
Tea, Coffee

LUNCH FOR A SPECIAL OCCASION

Mussel Soup
Coronation Chicken
Leeks with Brown Butter
Syllabub

A PLOUGHMAN'S LUNCH

Bread and Cheese
Pickled Onions
Beer

PUB FARE

Scotch Eggs
Cornish Pasties
Pickled Mushrooms
Rhubarb Crumble and Custard
Beer

A SUMMER PICNIC
Kipper Pâté
Veal, Ham and Egg Pie
Mango Chutney
Eton Mess
Cheese and Oatcakes
Cider

SUNDAY DINNER

Roast Beef and Yorkshire Pudding
Horseradish Sauce
Roast Potatoes
Braised Parsnips
Gooseberry Fool and Shortbread

AFTERNOON TEA

Scones
Cucumber Sandwiches
Brandy Snaps
Bosworth Jumbles
Old-Fashioned Walnut Cake
Tea

HIGH TEA

Crumpets
Banana Tea Loaf
Richmond Maids of Honor
Victoria Sponge
Toad in the Hole
Cheese
Tea

A SPICY SUPPER

Mulligatawny Soup
Fried Chicken with Gubbins Sauce
Spiced Cabbage
Mango Chutney
Flummery

CHRISTMAS DINNER

Roast Goose with Sage and Onion Stuffing
Plum Sauce
Brussels Sprouts with Chestnuts
Pan Haggerty
Mrs. Messenger's Christmas Plum Pudding
Brandy Butter
Mince Pies

A NEW YEAR'S EVE BUFFET

Potted Shrimps
Marbled Veal
Hindle Wakes
Sherried Puree of Peas
Trifle
Cheese

Index

ABOUT THE AUTHOR

Having lived in Paris and New York, JANE GARMEY nevertheless remembers well a childhood filled with glorious British food. Astonished by this country's lack of appreciation for her native cuisine, she decided "something must be done." Before setting pen to paper, she traveled expensively throughout the British Isles searching out indigenous recipes, sampling authentic cooking and discovering that many a continental delight was actually an English dish in disguise. Herself an accomplished cook, she has among other things worked in public television, reviewed films, founded a day-care center and directed an experimental fieldwork program for the City University of New York. She lives with her husband and son in New York City.